RECOMMENDATION WHETHER TO CONFISCATE, DESTROY AND BURN ALL JEWISH BOOKS

A Classic Treatise
against Anti-Semitism

Studies in
Judaism and Christianity

*Exploration of Issues in the
Contemporary Dialogue Between
Christians and Jews*

Editor in Chief for
Stimulus Books
Helga Croner

Editors
Lawrence Boadt, C.S.P.
Helga Croner
Rabbi Leon Klenicki
Kevin A. Lynch, C.S.P.
Dennis McManus

A STIMULUS BOOK

RECOMMENDATION WHETHER TO CONFISCATE, DESTROY AND BURN ALL JEWISH BOOKS

A Classic Treatise against Anti-Semitism

Johannes Reuchlin

Translated, Edited and with a Foreword by Peter Wortsman

Critical Introduction by Elisheva Carlebach

A STIMULUS BOOK

PAULIST PRESS ◆ NEW YORK ◆ MAHWAH, N.J.

Originally published as part of *Doctor Johannsen Reuchlins Augenspiegel,* published by Thomas Anshelm, Tübingen, Germany, 1511; and in modern German translation as *Gutachten über das Jüdische Schrifttum,* herausgegeben und übersetzt von Antonie Leinz-v. Dessauer. Published by Jan Thorbecke Verlag, Konstanz, Stuttgart, Germany, 1965.

Cover design by A. Michael Velthaus

Library of Congress Cataloging-in-Publication Data

Reuchlin, Johannes.
    [Gutachten über das Jüdische Schrifttum, English]
    Recommendation whether to confiscate, destroy and burn all Jewish books : a classic treatise against anti-semitism/by Johannes Reuchlin ; translator and foreword: Peter Wortsman.
       p. cm.—(Stimulus series)
    Includes bibliographical references.
    ISBN 0-8091-3972-3 (alk. paper)
    1. Christianity and other religions—Judaism—Early works to 1800. 2. Judaism—Relations—Christianity—Early works to 1800. 3. Jewish literature—Censorship—Early works to 1800. 4. Book burning—Early works to 1800. I. Title. II. Series.

BM535 .R46 2000
261.2′6—dc21

                                        00-038511

Published by Paulist Press
997 Macarthur Boulevard
Mahwah, New Jersey 07430

www.paulistpress.com

Printed and bound in the
United States of America

Contents

*This translation is dedicated
to the memory of the late Dr. Stefanie Isser,
a wise woman of the law.*

*The translator would also like to thank Dr. Paul Becker, professor
emeritus of German language and literature at New York Univer-
sity, for introducing him to the work of Johannes Reuchlin; and
Father Lawrence Boadt for shepherding the manuscript into print.*

Foreword

To the modern reader, Johannes Reuchlin's *Recommendation whether to confiscate, destroy and burn all Jewish books* is a stirring response to a preposterous question. It is difficult today to fathom the fact that this modest little text written in the first decade of the sixteenth century succeeded in stilling raging tongues of fire that in our own time fed so furiously on books and people.

I
WHY BURN BOOKS?

In the years 1507–9, a recently converted Jew, a butcher named Johannes Pfefferkorn, alleged in various pamphlets that all Jewish writings contain profanities and attacks against the Christian faith. It is highly unlikely that the butcher, who knew neither Hebrew (the language of the allegedly defamatory books) nor Latin (the language of his published attacks), could on his own accord have conceived the idea of so maligning his former brethren and their most precious possession, their books. Pfefferkorn had the active support of important members of the Dominican order in Cologne, who saw in him a willing tool to help spread the flames of the Inquisition that in 1492 had lapped up the last remnants of Jewish life and culture in Spain. (The butcher later landed a comfortable sinecure as director of a Dominican hospice.)

With the help of the friars, Pfefferkorn managed in the winter of 1509–10 to bring his case to a court of inquiry before Emperor Maximilian I. The emperor issued a decree ordering local magistrates throughout his realm to confiscate Jewish books so as to study their contents (a formidable task, considering the fact that none of the authorities so charged knew a word of Hebrew). After the emperor's mandate had already been carried out in a few places (in Frankfurt am Main, for instance), he inexplicably changed his mind and issued a second decree staying the execution of the first until such time as the allegations could be thoroughly considered. Influential Jews at court may well have raised protest. It is altogether possible that Maximilian had no serious intention of pursuing an inquiry in this matter and merely wished to accord his earlier decision an appearance of legality.

In June 1510, the emperor ordered his lord high chancellor, the Archbishop of Mainz, to solicit expert legal opinions from knowledgeable persons. Two of the individuals called upon to offer their opinions were Jakob van Hoogstraeten, grand inquisitor of Cologne (whose foregone conclusions in the matter favored the Pfefferkorn cause) and Johannes Reuchlin, professor of law.

Why did the emperor's lord high chancellor turn to a legal scholar and philologist from Pforzheim for a theological opinion? Johannes Reuchlin (1455–1522) was known at court as one of the foremost jurists and legal scholars of his day. He was also a humanist, an enlightened thinker and, like his friend Erasmus of Rotterdam, an impassioned student of classical philology and philosophy. At age twenty, he published a Latin dictionary, *Vocabularius breviloquus* (1475).

Reuchlin shared with other humanists an interest in ancient Greek and completed notable translations from Greek into Latin. He became famous in humanist circles with his *De Rudimentis Hebraicis* (1506), the first dependable Hebrew grammar written by a Christian scholar in Latin.

How is it that a pious Christian like Reuchlin took the trouble to delve into a linguistic domain that had long been considered at best obsolete by most of his contemporaries? For just as the Jews themselves were reviled as a people who in rejecting Christ had missed the boat, an alien body that had long since outlived its usefulness, so too was their language and literary heritage, though for the most part unknown, held in ill repute. Reuchlin himself, it should be noted, was no particular friend of the Jews, whom he, like other enlightened Christians of his day, hoped to convert to the "true faith" by "reasonable" (i.e., noncoercive) means through debate and disputation. He was, however, an enthusiastic student of their sacred literature, for in it he saw the spiritual foundation of Christianity.

The Kabbalah: Mysticism of Language

Like other itinerant northern European humanists of his day drawn by the classical cultural currents preserved and fostered to the south, Reuchlin took several trips to Italy, where the study of Latin and Greek literature was enjoying a new blossoming of interest. A small intellectual elite led a relatively open exchange of ideas under the patronage of enlightened lords and clerics, a discussion in which, to a limited extent, Jewish notions and Jewish scholars were also included. Christian philosophers like Marsilio Ficino and Pico della Mirandola (both of whom Reuchlin met and befriended) knew and read ancient Hebrew. They developed in their thinking a curious synthesis of Christian doctrine, neoplatonic concepts and ideas drawn from the Jewish mystical tradition of the Kabbalah.

The word *kabbalah* means tradition. The roots of this tradition, the ideas and kernels of meaning upon which the Kabbalah is based, derive from the Old Testament and its commentaries. The Jewish faith and the traditional Hebrew books constitute a unity: Word and truth are one. The Kabbalah as a discrete system of beliefs and practices is in fact a more recent development. The *Zohar,* one of the central kabbalist texts, was most likely first written down in the thirteenth century. In subsequent centuries, kabbalistic ideas spread throughout Europe and the Middle East. In Spain, Provence and Germany important schools were founded. In Safed, a small hill town in the heart of what today is Israel, one of the most important kabbalistic schools grew in the sixteenth century around a core group of mystical thinkers and teachers. From there, students and ideas wandered back to Europe.

For the kabbalists (Jewish and Christian alike), the Hebrew language itself held a sacred significance. For it was with Hebrew words that the Judeo-Christian God quite literally *called* the world into being. Each word passed on to man through the Bible, the kabbalists believed, is a muttering echo and shimmering mirror image of "the eternal." The Hebrew language as such is a bridge, a lasting link between God and man. Among other practices, the kabbalists developed a system of mystical meditation on the numerical value and metaphysical significance of Hebrew letters and words.

Christian students of the Kabbalah, like Ficino, Pico della Mirandola and Reuchlin, perceived in it a confirmation of Christian mystical doctrine. What united the Christian and

Jewish kabbalists, despite their considerable theological differences, was the desire to approach God (the Eternal); they saw Hebrew as the living language of God, and as such, the sacred structure of creation, the very foundation of "eternal truth."

II
REUCHLIN'S *RECOMMENDATION:* TWO PARALLEL CONCEPTS OF TRUTH

It is the task of a jurist to establish and prove the veracity or falsehood of allegations by discrediting rumors, superstitions, slander and outright lies and demonstrating the guilt or innocence of the accused in relation to the charge. Such a task naturally requires a thorough knowledge of the law and an inordinately logical, rational manner of thinking, not to speak of rhetorical skills. At the same time, the tendency to believe in the provability of guilt or innocence bespeaks a firm conviction that such a thing as truth exists at all.

Like every great scholarly or poetic work, Johannes Reuchlin's *Recommendation Whether...Jewish Books* can be read in retrospect on at least two levels. From the standpoint of its historical significance, this work is first and foremost a masterpiece of jurisprudence, a classical example of legal rigor and critical reason. The second level on which Reuchlin's *Recommendation* can be read (a level, moreover, that cannot be separated from its legal purpose and style, but rather rests upon it as moss upon a rock) is metaphysical. For Reuchlin the jurist was simultaneously Reuchlin the kabbalist, and what he wrote is also a moving meditation on the mystery of language.

True or False

In response to the question, "Should the Jews' books be legally confiscated, destroyed or burned?" one could sum up Reuchlin's answer in brief: Do not burn what you do not understand!

He begins with an overview of the charges brought against the Jewish books: that they "…were written to counter the Christians"; that they malign "Jesus, Mary…the Apostles…and our Christian Order"; that they "are false"; that they induce "the Jews…to stubbornly cling to Judaism."

In response to such claims, he argues: that "the Jews…have a right to protection under the Imperial Law"; that "according to Imperial and Royal laws, no one may by forceful means [be relieved of] his property"; that "every individual is assured the right to [retain] his…practices, customs and property"; that "such books were never repudiated or condemned either by canonical or secular law…."

Reuchlin proceeds thereafter to enumerate the various kinds of Jewish books under consideration: "the Holy Scripture" (i.e., the twenty-four books of the Hebrew Bible); "the Talmud" (i.e., the commentaries); "the glosses and comments…concerning individual books of the Bible"; "sermons, disputations and prayer books," "philosophical and scholarly works of all sorts"; and finally, "poetic works, fables, poems, fairy tales, satires and collections of instructive exempla." By outlining in brief the nature of each of the aforementioned kinds of books, he succeeds in his primary objective, which is to tear away the veil of strangeness and the pall of superstition surrounding these books in the popular consciousness.

In the last-mentioned category, "poetic works," he concedes the possibility that certain books may indeed contain scornful references to Christianity. "Of these," Reuchlin writes, "each book has its own title, just as the author conceived it." A poetic work, he reminds, is the individual expression of its author and not necessarily representative of the collective voice of his people.

Reuchlin's presentation is so straightforward and his argument so airtight and reasonable that even the most fiery of his opponents would have been hard-pressed to find fault. Paraphrasing Aristotle, Reuchlin asserts that:

> A wise man should possess two qualities, namely the following: that he not lie, and that he be able to counter that which is the stuff of lies.

Consequently:

> He must not fly into a rage and burn the books if he has not studied enough to oppose them with reasoned arguments in sermons or debates.

And wisely citing irrefutable ecclesiastical sources in support of his premise, he quotes St. Jerome:

> But how can anyone oppose that which he does not understand?

And back to Aristotle, to reiterate the obvious:

> Whoever knows not the meaning of words and of their language easily errs in his interpretation.

From which Reuchlin logically concludes:

> How then can we countenance that the Christians reject the Talmud, which they do not even understand?

To illustrate his legal point Reuchlin taps his linguistic expertise, demonstrating how in a few instances the unschooled reader might misconstrue the meaning of a text in a foreign tongue. Among other examples, he shows that the Hebrew term for "all those who do not abide by the true faith" cannot possibly be taken as a derogatory slander against the Christians, as had been suggested, "since the Jews pray with the same words throughout the whole world, wherever they may live," that is, not only in Christendom.

With a single comparison, he effectively crushes and ridicules the very premise of his opponents' position:

> If someone wished to write against the mathematicians and were himself ignorant in simple arithmetic or mathematics, he would be made a laughing stock.

And to dispel any possible lingering doubt, Reuchlin points to the lack of historical precedent for such a wanton act of destruction:

> For had it been deemed necessary to burn the Talmud then it would have been burned many centuries ago, since our ancestors were after all so much more zealous in matters of Christian faith than we.

What pious Dominican would have the gall to question the wisdom and challenge the authority of the church fathers?

Even St. Augustine, Reuchlin notes, lashed out at the many bad, that is, faulty, translations of the Holy Scripture in his day:

> The precise meaning of the Holy Scripture can only be understood according to the unique qualities of each language in which it is written. For each language has its own particular mode of expression unique to itself. If this [mode of expression] is taken literally in its

translation into another language, it would appear to anyone reading it that the words made no sense at all....

Reuchlin is adamant when it comes to linguistic ignorance. "With all due respect," he prefaces a sharp counterattack against his opponents, adding insult to injury,

one can find many Christian scholars who because of their ignorance of these two languages [Hebrew and Greek] cannot rightly explain [the Scripture] and in this are often made a laughing stock.

In his appreciation of the work of Hebrew scholars, constituting some of the books in question, Reuchlin earned himself the lifelong enmity of countless scholastics and theologians of his day:

Therefore should we by no means suppress the commentaries and glosses of those who have thoroughly mastered their mother tongue, having studied it since their youth, but rather wherever such commentaries exist we should make them accessible, take pains to preserve them and hold them in high esteem as sources from which flow the true meaning of the language and the significance of the Holy Scripture.

It must be reiterated here that, despite his admiration for their scholarship, Reuchlin is not concerned with the protection of the Jewish people per se, but rather of Jewish books, which he considered the foundation of Christian culture. And yet, though he was not a friend of the Jews, Reuchlin's sense of justice and truth was nevertheless greater than any anti-Jewish sentiments he may have shared.

In answer to the question of whether the Jewish books were essentially "false," that is, "untrue," Reuchlin insists:

> And even if in this regard the Jewish books may be false, according to our way of thinking, they are not false according to their [the Jews'] way of thinking and according to their faith.

Reuchlin finds fault with the very allegation of falsity and proceeds by elimination (in an attempt to establish a legal definition of the term), to peel away the layers of prejudice and ignorance that underlie the allegation. If "false" means "faulty," then:

> ...the first scribe of the Holy Gospel According to Matthew likewise erred and made mistakes in his transcription....For if the [Jewish] books would have to be burned for that reason, namely because they were not transcribed and copied accurately, then we would have to burn many copies of the Holy Bible....[For] they are all based on the immaculate Jewish original text.

And further, regarding the alleged "falseness" of the books in question:

> If "false" means a deliberate suppression or alteration of the truth with malicious intent,...then I know of no people on earth that takes greater pains to assure accuracy in copying the Holy Scripture than do the Jews.

Finally, the linguist and the jurist join forces:

> But...if a [Jewish] scholar, who interprets the Scripture to the best of his abilities, as he sees it, the result being conclusive or not, in so doing he is committing

no fraud…, then no law or statute can justify that such
books be burned.

False in the legal sense, means "having false [i.e.,
fraudulent] intent," and that precisely is what Reuchlin
demonstrates the accused Jewish books are not; and therefore, they most definitely do not deserve to be burned.

"The Eternal Truth"

In the Judeo-Christian tradition, language itself plays a
key role. Language is not merely a social mode of communication; it is the echo and everlasting receptacle of the primal syllables with which God spoke the world into being,
and as such, man's only access to the sacred syntax of creation.

And God said, "Let there be light"; and there was
light.

In creating man, God accorded him a limited (re-
creative) linguistic talent: the ability to assign names to the
things God made:

…and whatsoever Adam called every living creature,
that was the name thereof.

And though we mortals are not, it is true, endowed with the
virtuoso rhetorical skills of the celestial Speaker who
uttered us into being, like children, we create sentences by
parroting the words of the creation.

In the New Testament reinterpretation of the creation
(The Gospel According to St. John), our beginnings slip
back even closer to the Ur-mouth:

> In the beginning was the Word, and the Word was with God, and the Word was God.

Here language and God, the primal speaker, are one. But what dialect does he speak?

For Reuchlin, who was both a pious Christian and a convinced kabbalist, there could be no question in this regard: Hebrew is the language of God, and therefore, the Jewish books under attack constitute unquestionable "testimony to the eternal truth"—a truth whose opposite is not a lie, but rather the incoherent chaos that preceded the creation. If human history is a collection of divine invocations, as Reuchlin and his fellow kabbalists believed, then the Jewish books comprise a record and bridge over time binding the past to the transitory present and preserving it for eternity. For Reuchlin, the Jews themselves were not so much a living people as the archivists of our common heritage, or as he puts it:

> For the Jews are in a certain sense our Capsarii, bookkeepers and librarians, who preserve for us those books from which we may derive proof for our faith....

On the eve of the Reformation, launched some seven years later by a monk named Martin Luther (an early follower of Reuchlin's), religious faith was a fundamental tenet of sixteenth-century thought. To Reuchlin, faith is grounded in reason and sired not by crude coercion but by the free and open exchange of ideas. "Belief comes from listening," he writes. And ideas are transmitted by the sacred vessel of language:

> For Christ's word comes into the ears and through the ears into the heart and from the heart into the will and

through the will it crystallizes into conviction—and from this derives faith.

Language then, the word as deed and testimony to that deed preserved in sacred books, has the power to move stubborn hearts and minds to accept the truth. True faith, however, Reuchlin firmly believed, cannot be imposed; and herein lies the justice of the man: for though he viewed the Jewish faith as wrong or misguided, he nevertheless supported the right of the Jewish people to adhere to it:

> ...for as to matters of faith, they [the Jews] are of the opinion that their faith is right and ours is wrong. Indeed, we find among certain Jews the view that every nation ought to be allowed to practice its own faith; and just as we are not bound by the Laws of Moses, so they are not subject to the laws of Jesus; rather, they are bound to comply with Moses' laws, for God gave them to the Jews and to no one else...and all that follows from those laws constitutes their faith: and in their practices, they wish to injure no one.

Finally, as the ultimate substantiation of his position, Reuchlin avows:

> ...I rest my argument upon the Holy Gospel itself. For our Lord Jesus Christ said to the Jews (John 5,39): "Search the Scriptures; for in them ye think ye have eternal life: and they are they which testify of me."

This Reuchlin calls "the foundation...of my defense."

Jurist-linguist-Christian-kabbalist, Johannes Reuchlin strove for a transcendent all-encompassing concept of truth, the terrestrial as well as the eternal. We heirs to the colossal lies of the twentieth century, whose ideological bonfires consumed people and books, find it hard to even entertain a notion of "eternal truth." We have been schooled in eternal doubt; such certainty is quite simply alien to our way of thinking—we lack the capacity to believe, and yet like amputees we continue to kick as if we had it, in the vain hope perhaps that if we kick enough it might someday grow back.

> ...from this we may conclude that their books must not be taken from them by force, for books are as dear to some as their children. Do we not in our common usage follow the parlance of the poets, for whom the books they write are in a manner of speaking children (of the soul).
>
> —Johannes Reuchlin, 1510

Critical Introduction

Johannes Reuchlin (1455–1522) has been justly cele-brated as one of the extraordinary intellectual figures of the northern European Renaissance, along with Erasmus of Rotterdam and other German Reformation figures. Reuch-lin's intellectual world was shaped by several developments in the late fifteenth and early sixteenth centuries. In the late fifteenth century, he studied in Florence and absorbed the extraordinary influence of the humanist circles around Mar-silio Ficino and Pico della Mirandola. From them he learned to value both the Greek and Hebrew patrimony of Western civilization. When he returned to German lands, Reuchlin became aware of the gap between the advances in humanis-tic knowledge made in Italy and the status of German humanism. Aware that the Germans lagged far behind their Italian counterparts, he advocated the study of Hebrew, along with Greek and Latin, as a prerequisite for any authentic encounter with the texts that formed the basis for Christian civilization. Reuchlin was the first competent Christian Hebraist in German lands, and he pioneered meth-ods of using Kabbalah, Jewish mystical teachings, to sup-port Christian doctrines.

Another important factor in Reuchlin's career was the spread of inexpensive printing throughout German cities by the early sixteenth century. Ideas could be disseminated far more broadly than in the age of hand-written manuscripts. While most laypeople could not read, both Reuchlin and his opponents were aware of the great power of this new medium. Many of the texts on both sides of the Reuchlin controversy were printed in the German vernacular rather than in Latin. This would enable them to reach as many readers as possible. In this respect, Reuchlin's controversy adumbrates the career of Martin Luther, whose success is unimaginable without taking the effects of printing into account.

Reuchlin's exalted place in both western European and Jewish history stems from his pivotal role in the controversy over Jewish books. Reuchlin's nemesis was a recent convert from Judaism, Johannes Pfefferkorn. Pfefferkorn published several treatises beginning in 1507, all of them abusive toward the Jewish religion and tradition. He called for an accelerated program of missionizing designed to bring about the mass conversion of Jews in German lands. Among his recommendations were economic restrictions on Jewish livelihood, the coercion of Jews to attend Christian sermons and the destruction of Jewish books. It was the latter recommendation that would light a spark of controversy among the learned men of the empire and set Reuchlin and Pfefferkorn on a collision course.

Pfefferkorn repeated accusations based on a Christian polemical tradition of misunderstanding how Jews read the Talmud and misrepresenting its contents. He presented all postbiblical Jewish literature as though it were one combined genre, all of it deeply anti-Christian in nature. In fact, the Talmud itself was composed over hundreds of years and contains material in legal, moralistic, narrative and imaginative modes. Jews related to the different types of writing in different ways. Indeed, except for two medieval volumes of patently anti-Christian polemic (*Toledot Yeshu* and the anonymous medieval *Nizzahon*) most of the Jewish literature under discussion barely showed any interest in Christianity at all. This did not deter Pfefferkorn and his supporters, who were determined to eradicate the presence of Jews and Judaism from German lands.

Prodded by Pfefferkorn and the Dominicans of Cologne, Emperor Maximilian I (d. 1519) ordered the confiscation of Jewish books in some cities of the empire. The confiscations had already begun when the Jews appealed to the emperor to reconsider. He ordered that opinions on the question of Jewish books be rendered by several theological faculties, as well as several well-known individuals. Of all the literature generated by the emperor's mandate, the voice of Johannes Reuchlin stands alone for its bold content and calm tone. It was the intention of the instigators to undermine the civil status of Jews within the empire by depicting them as dangerous enemies of Christians who should be deprived of the right to live anywhere in Christendom. In their view, the only justification for the continued existence of Jews among Christians was their conversion. They argued that this much-anticipated conversion of the Jews to Christianity was impeded by their books, particularly the Talmud. Pfefferkorn described all Jewish books as blasphemous anti-Christian tracts that ought to be confiscated and burned. In articulating these views, Pfefferkorn built upon a strong medieval anti-Jewish monastic tradition and appears to have been aided by certain Dominicans at Cologne. They used the former Jew to lend greater credibility to their anti-Jewish evaluations.

Reuchlin's *Recommendation* responded to these charges by addressing two fundamental and related issues:

the place of Jews in Christian society and his prescription for the role of Jewish books within the Christian world. As a product of sixteenth-century Christian society, Reuchlin certainly saw Jews through theological lenses, but his vision differed from that of many of his contemporaries. While Reuchlin believed that Christianity superseded Judaism and Christian society should seek to convert Jews, Reuchlin rejected every vestige of force. Jews had a right to practice their religion within the framework of the empire long before the birth of Christianity. From the point of view of imperial law, both religions were "sects," and their adherents were equally subject to the laws of the empire. Reuchlin reached back to the image of the multiethnic and multireligious Roman Empire that preceded the rise of Christianity. Reuchlin argued that measures such as book burning or the kidnapping of Jewish children for the purpose of being raised as Christians—any resort to coercive measures whatsoever—should be shunned. Gentle persuasion and the force of reason were the only acceptable means of gaining converts. Reuchlin believed that true converts gained in the right manner, even though few in number, were much more valuable to Christendom than masses of reluctant or forced adherents.

Reuchlin's statement, "There is no people on earth that accords them [the Jews] greater freedom and welcomes them more readily than do the Christians, as we may find affirmed in canonical and secular law," may have produced a chuckle among his readers (Wortsman translation, 43). No person reading these lines in the early sixteenth century could have remained unaware that Jewish communities throughout Europe, including many in cities in the German lands, had recently been uprooted by a sweeping series of expulsions of Jews from places where they had been living peacefully for centuries. None could have been unaware that Jews were subjected to a relentless and capricious campaign to depict them as demonic murderers and desecrators of Christian sancta. In the very year that Reuchlin wrote his *Recommendation,* 1510, thirty-eight Jews had been burned in Berlin on charges that they had stolen and tortured a host, although a Christian blacksmith had earlier confessed to the theft. In 1511, the same year that Reuchlin published his *Recommendation,* an elaborate book was published in German about this Jewish "crime," complete with many details, court proceedings and twenty-five illustrations. Even if only for the purpose of winning their hearts for Christianity, Reuchlin agreed with the sentiments expressed by Luther in his essay, "That Jesus Christ was born a Jew," [1523] "For they have dealt with the Jews as if they were dogs and not human beings....If I had been a Jew, I would sooner have been a sow than a Christian." Reuchlin was first to indicate the gap that existed between the rights of Jews acknowledged by both church and state and the increasing violation of those rights in the Christian world.

As a legal opinion, Reuchlin's treatise illuminates the struggle between Roman, canon and customary law in early modern German lands. Maximilian I, the emperor, had been trying to restore the rule of Roman law over the land and wanted to reclaim powers that had been ceded to the church over the centuries. Reuchlin appealed to precisely this ambition of Maximilian's. By arguing that the Jews belonged to the "empire" and fell under its laws as any other subjects, Reuchlin was implying that the church had no legal right to exercise power over Jewish beliefs or property. Reuchlin argued that only persons who had once embraced Christianity and later repudiated its doctrines could be considered heretics by the church. Reuchlin was reversing centuries of church encroachment into the territory of Jewry law by arguing that Jews simply did not fall under the church's jurisdiction. If Christians found anything published by Jews to be slanderous of their religion, they had recourse to the courts, where Jews could be sued for libel like anyone else (Wortsman translation, 36–37). Reuchlin's voice for the rule of justice and law in an age of seething religious hostility may be one of the earliest arguments for the separation of church and state.

As for the facts concerning the content of Jewish books, Reuchlin mocked Pfefferkorn's pretensions. He correctly pointed out that no Christians then living in German lands, himself included, and few Jews, could claim any kind of competency in Talmud. He distinguished among the various genres of Jewish literature and pointed out that many of the books in question referred to pagans rather than Christians; that very few Jewish books were devoted to the subject of refuting Christianity directly. The books were necessary for Jews to teach them how to observe their religion properly, and neither church nor state had a right to interfere in this internal Jewish process.

The Reuchlin controversy has often been characterized by scholars as a struggle between the tolerant and enlightened forces of "humanism" against the obscurantist clerical forces of "scholasticism." This model for the controversy was already propounded while it still raged, when Ulrich von Hutten published his *Epistolae obscurum virorum (Letters of Obscure Men),* a satirical parody of the anti-Reuchlin forces which skewered their obscurantism and located it in the scholastic tradition. This view is not consistent with the virulent anti-Judaism of most of the "humanist" figures and Reformation leaders. It was Erasmus who said, "If it is Christian to hate the Jews, then are we not all excellent Christians?"

Many humanists, even those who shared Reuchlin's appreciation of Hebrew, expressed only loathing for Jews and supported the most inhumane treatment of them. Of all the scholars who were asked an opinion concerning the fate of Jewish books, only Reuchlin expressed a positive viewpoint. The anti-Jewish attitudes and policies of Reformers such as Martin Luther and Martin Bucer are well known. It is also important to note that throughout his forceful arguments Reuchlin never advocated a break from the Catholic Church. He appealed to the tradition of fairness, reason and due process, while his opponents emphasized the zealous inquisitorial spirit ever in search of new targets to pursue for heresy, witchcraft and perfidy. It is no happenstance that some of the important voices raised in the following generation in support of decent treatment of Jews in German lands were those of Reuchlin's disciples, Andreas Osiander, Phillip Melanchthon and Wolfgang Capito.

Scholars have often commented that Reuchlin was no friend of the Jewish people, that he had earlier expressed inimical opinions concerning Jews, that he too believed they ought to be converted and that he merely wished to save the books for their theological and scholarly value. It is unclear what Reuchlin's deepest personal feelings toward his Jewish contemporaries were. His positive opinions concerning Jews and their books may have been based on his respectful relationship with his own teachers of Hebrew and Jewish texts. He had studied with Emperor Frederick III's Jewish court physician, Jacob Loans, and with Obadiah Seforno, a noted Italian-Jewish biblical exegete. On the other hand, if Reuchlin's earlier writing reflected a personal aversion to Jews, the firm voice in the *Recommendation* concerning the rights of Jews to protection under the law and the value of

Jewish writings for Christian men of learning was all the more remarkable. In any case, Reuchlin's *Recommendation* was about as close as any prominent person in his time could come in defense of Jewish interests without seriously jeopardizing his livelihood and even his life.

In 1511, Reuchlin published his *Recommendation,* along with several other supporting documents, in a pamphlet he called *Augenspiegel.* After its publication, Reuchlin was branded a heretic by his opponents, and a torrent of controversial pamphlets and tracts were unleashed by each side. The controversy raged for a decade. In 1513, Jacob Hoogstraeten, head of the Inquisition in Cologne, began inquisitorial proceedings against Reuchlin's opinions. By 1514 he succeeded in doing to Reuchlin's writing what he had not succeeded in doing to Jewish books—they were condemned to be burned at the stake. The controversy shifted away from its initial subject, the question of Jewish books, to the question of whether Reuchlin could be charged with heresy for his position. Several theological faculties argued that the very act of reopening for debate the question of burning Jewish books, which had already been approved by two medieval popes, was a heretical step on Reuchlin's part. By debating the question Reuchlin was casting doubt on the competency of those popes who had approved it in the past, thereby strengthening the Jews in their stubbornness. In 1516 the pope, Leo X, set a date to proceed against Reuchlin. His works were ultimately condemned by the pope in 1520. Reuchlin died in 1522. Reuchlin's arguments had broken new ground with their dispassionate examination of a subject fraught with intense emotion.

The attack against Jewish books orchestrated by Pfefferkorn and the Dominicans at Cologne was only an early salvo in what the Dominicans envisioned as a long and bitter campaign to rid German Christian society of its Jewish coresidents. Fresh from their triumph of the 1490s, in which the Jews of Iberia were expelled under terrible circumstances, the Dominicans, who had engineered that expulsion after centuries of pressure on Iberian Jews, were now looking toward the German lands of the empire to expand their campaign to make Europe homogeneously Christian. It is impossible to argue whether they would have been ultimately successful had their efforts not been abruptly thwarted, first by the calm reason of Reuchlin and later by the eruption of Luther's Reformation, which gave them plenty of other problems. Historian Richard Kieckheffer has argued that German society was so politically fragmented in the medieval period that it could never have become home to an efficient heresy-hunting bureaucracy. Yet the attempt to destroy the Jewish books throughout the empire nearly succeeded. With the aid of the city council and representatives of the clergy, Pfefferkorn succeeded in having 168 manuscripts removed from the Frankfurt am Main synagogue on September 28, 1509. In the spring of 1510, another 1500 volumes were confiscated. At the same time, Jewish books were also confiscated in Mainz, Bingen, Lorch, Lahnstein and Deutz. If the wholesale destruction of Jewish books would have followed, as seemed inevitable, it would have impaired the ability of Jews to function as a community. It would likely have caused irreparable disruption to their religious and intellectual lives.

It is no wonder that Jewish contemporaries of Reuchlin viewed his position as heroic and his intervention on their behalf as nothing short of miraculous. Although contemporary historians often feel obliged to explain and apologize for Reuchlin's negative statements concerning Jews, the most prominent Jew in the German Empire of his time lauded Reuchlin as a hero. "Our enemies, and the oppressors from among our own people [Pfefferkorn], arose to abolish the written Torah; then God demonstrated a double miracle to us, for the Torah was returned to its former glory [the books were returned] by a sage among the nations [Reuchlin]." * Josel of Rosheim, spokesman for Jews of the German Empire, and a direct observer of the events, penned this description of the Reuchlin-Pfefferkorn controversy in the first half of the sixteenth century.

For Josel and other German Jews, the confiscation aroused a host of sorrowful historical memories of earlier cycles of denunciation and book burning that had destroyed significant portions of the Jewish literary patrimony. The pattern became a familiar one in medieval Christendom. A convert from Judaism, sometimes acting independently and sometimes as a front for Christian clerics, "exposed" the material embedded in a Jewish text that could be interpreted as offensive to Christianity. The Christian authorities then investigated the charges and if deemed true, would order the large-scale confiscation and burning of the offending texts. A classical example was the trial, denunciation, confiscation and burning of the Talmud in 1242. In 1236, convert from Judaism Nicholas Donin brought a list of charges against Jewish books to the attention of Pope Gregory IX. Three years later, the pope sent a directive to the kings and bishops of France, England, Spain and Portugal commanding that the books of the Jews be confiscated on the first Sabbath of Lent, March 3, 1240. Books containing doctrinal errors would be condemned to be burned at the stake. The only

---

*Josel of Rosheim, "Chronicle," in Hava-Fraenkel Goldschmidt, ed. *Josel of Rosheim: Historical Writings* (Hebrew) (Jerusalem, 1996), 285.

king to comply fully with the directive was Louis IX of France. In 1242, over twenty wagon loads of Jewish manuscripts, tens of thousands of irreplaceable volumes, were burned in Paris. This became a classic pattern in medieval Christian Europe.

As the Jewish communities were systematically pressured by clerical, papal and royal powers, the deprivation of the books necessary to sustain the inner life of the People of the Book became a standard feature of their oppression. The fourteenth century saw the Talmud burned in Bourges, Toulouse, Paris, Pamiers and Rome. Dominican and Franciscan friars played a leading role in the drive to eliminate Jewish books. When the Dominicans began to turn their attention to German lands after their victory in Spain and Portugal, where Jewish life had been entirely effaced, German Jews had every reason to fear for their precious books and, eventually, for their very existence.

That a Christian "sage" would arise to refute the charges leveled by a convert from Judaism was an unprecedented turn of events. Was Reuchlin being disingenuous when he remarked, "For if the Talmud should have been torched, surely it would have been fed to the flames many centuries ago…never indeed as far as I can recall, have I read any such suggestion or wish expressed by those who criticize the Talmud…" (Wortsman translation, 46). Surely a man of Reuchin's erudition knew the fate of the Talmud in earlier ages. Indeed, he explicitly referred to that event in his *Defensio,* published at the same time as the *Recommendation.* Yet he maintained that Pfefferkorn's suggestion was an outrageous innovation. Once the tide had been turned, Jewish books in German lands were saved. To Josel of Rosheim, keenly aware of the outcome of earlier controversies, it seemed nothing less than miraculous.

Until the publication of this translation into English by Peter Wortsman, Reuchlin's remarkable affirmation of the right of Jews to live alongside Christians as *"concives"*— cocitizens of the Roman Empire—his pioneering defense of Jewish books has not been accessible to English readers. Precious few documents penned in the sixteenth century refer to *"uns"* and *"unser"* ("we"/"our," Wortsman translation, 36) placing Jew alongside Christian as part of the universe of discourse of legal and humane rights. Reuchlin's courageous and unique words deserve the wider audience this translation will bring them.

Bibliography of Works Relating to Reuchlin-Pfefferkorn Controversy

Ben-Sasson, Hayim Hillel. "Jewish-Christian Disputation in the Setting of Humanism and Reformation in the German Empire," *Harvard Theological Review* 59(1966): 369–90.

Breuer, Mordechai. "The Early Modern Period," in Michael A. Meyer, ed., *German-Jewish History in Modern Times*. New York: 1996. 1:57–65.

Cohen, Jeremy. *The Friars and the Jews: The Evolution of Medieval Anti-Judaism*. Ithaca: 1982.

Fraenkel-Goldschmidt, Hava, ed. *Josel of Rosheim: Historical Writings* (Hebrew). Jerusalem: 1996. 108–12, 285.

Freudenthal, M. "Dokumente zur Schriftverfolgung durch Pfefferkorn," *Zeitschrift für die Geschichte der Juden in Deutschland* N.F. 3(1931): 228ff.

Friedman, Jerome. *The Most Ancient Testimony: Sixteenth Century Christian-Hebraica in the Age of Renaissance Nostalgia*. Athens, Ohio: 1983.

Geiger, Ludwig. *Johannes Reuchlin-sein Leben und seine Werke*. Leipzig, 1871.

———. *Johann Reuchlins Briefwechsel*. Tübingen, 1875.

———. "Ein Beitrag zur Geschichte der Juden und zur Charakteristik des Reuchlin'schen Streites," *Geiger's Zeitschrift für Wissenschaft und Leben* 7(1869): 293–309.

———. "Die Juden und die deutsche Literatur, 4:Die Juden und die Literatur des 16. Jahrhunderts," *Zeitschrift für die Geschichte der Juden in Deutschland* 2(1888): 308–74.

Graetz, Heinrich. "Aktenstücke zur Confiscation der jüdischen Schriften in Frankfurt am Main unter Kaiser Maximilian durch Pfefferkorns Angeberei," *Monatsschrift für Geschichte und Wissenschaft des Judentums* 24 (1875): 289ff., 337ff.

Herzig, Arno and Schoeps, Julius H., eds. *Reuchlin und die Juden*. Sigmaringen, 1993.

Kedar, Benjamin. "Canon Law and the Burning of the Talmud," *Bulletin of Medieval Law* 9 (1979): 79–82.

Kirn, Hans-Martin. *Das Bild vom Juden im Deutschland des frühen 16. Jahrhunderts dargestellt an den Schriften Johannes Pfefferkorns*. Tübingen, 1989. [Contains a bibliography of all Pfefferkorn's printed works, 201–204].

Kracauer, Isidor. "Die Confiscation der hebraïschen Schriften in Frankfurt am Main in den Jahren 1509 und 1510," *ZGJD* 1(1887): 160–76; 2 (1888): 230–48.

———. "Actenstücke zur Geschichte der Confiscation der hebraïschen Schriften in Frankfurt am Main," *MGWJ* 44 (1900): 114–26, 167–77, 220–34.

———. "Verzeichnis der von Pfefferkorn 1510 in Frankfurt am Main confiscierten jüdischen Bücher," *MGWJ* 44 (1900): 114–26, 167–77, 220–34, 455–60.

———. *Geschichte der Juden in Frankfurt am Main* (Frankfurt, 1927) 1:238ff.

Oberman, Heiko. *The Roots of Anti-Semitism in the Age of Renaissance and Reformation.* Philadelphia, 1984.

———. "Three Sixteenth Century Attitudes to Judaism: Reuchlin, Erasmus and Luther," in Bernard D. Cooperman, ed., *Jewish Thought in the Sixteenth Century.* Cambridge, Mass., 1983.

Overfield, James H., "A New Look at the Reuchlin Affair," *Studies in Medieval and Renaissance History* 8(1971): 165–207.

Peterse, Hans. *Jacobus Hoogstraeten gegen Johannes Reuchlin: Ein Beitrag zur Geschichte des anti-Judaismus im 16. Jahrhundert.* Mainz, 1995.

Rembaum, Joel. "The Talmud and the Popes," *Viator* 13 (1982): 203–23.

Spitz, Lewis W. *The Religious Renaissance of the German Humanists,* Cambridge, Mass., 1963. 61–80.

Stokes, F. Griffin, transl. *Epistolae obscurum virorum.* London, 1909.

A Recommendation Whether to Confiscate, Destroy and Burn All Jewish Books

To His Serene Highness, the most noble Lord and Master, Master Uriel, Archbishop of Mainz, Chancellor and Elector of the Holy Roman Empire of the German Nation, My Lordship, I, Johannes Reuchlin of Pforzheim, Professor of Philosophy and Doctor of Imperial Law, do offer my eternally devoted and willing service. Your most gracious Lordship, gracious Sire!

As your obedient servant, I hereby acknowledge with profound reverence the receipt of the charge and order first issued to your Lordship by His Majesty, our most high Lord and Sire, Maximilian, Roman Emperor, and now passed on to me with a mandate to proceed accordingly; wherein I am asked to probe in a thorough manner and with all necessary care the matter of the confiscated or sequestered books which the Jews currently use in conjunction with the Laws of Moses, the Prophets and the Psalms of the Old Testament, and to recommend by what means and with what justification to approach the whole matter and to decide what is to be done. And in particular, I am asked to offer my recommendation on whether the destruction of said books would be pious, praise-

31

worthy and useful to our holy Christian Faith, and whether it would indeed be productive in promoting the service of God.

Though well aware that I am far too insignificant to comment on such weighty legal matters that concern the good of the Christian Church and the praise and honor of His Imperial Majesty, the Holy Roman Emperor, being duty bound, I would, nevertheless, rather be judged unwise than disobedient, and do, therefore, put herewith in writing my humble opinion regarding the following question:

Should or can the Jews' books be lawfully confiscated, destroyed or burned?

Some would say yes, for several reasons:

First: These books are written to oppose the Christians.

Further: They are offensive to Jesus, Maria and the Apostles, and to us and our Christian Order.

Third: They are false.

Fourth: Through them, the Jews are misled, and so induced to stubbornly cling to Judaism and not to convert to the Christian Faith.

Yet whosoever has it in his power to avert such a great iniquity and does not prevent or eliminate it, he is as guilty as the perpetrator and should, as an accessory to the crime, be held guilty and liable to the same punishment *(ex de off. de lega. c.1. et. i. q. 1. quicquid invisibilis).*

There are others, however, who would reply: No!, and they too have their reasons:

First: As subjects of the Holy Roman Empire, the Jews have recourse to protection under Imperial Law *(I. judaei communi romano jure. C. de judaeis).*

Further: Our possessions may not be taken from us without our compliance *(I. id quod nostrum. ff. de reg. Jure).*

Third: The Imperial and Royal Law as well as other sovereign statutes prescribe that no one may have his possessions confiscated by force *(I. 1. §. nequid autem. ff. de vi. et vi.).*

Fourth: Every one must be assured of his right to protection of his lawful practices, customs and property, even if he be a thief *(c. in literis de resti. spo. in fi.).*

Fifth: Thus the Jews must be permitted to maintain their synagogues, known as *Shuls,* in peace, without bother or interference *(c. 3. ex. de judaeis).*

Sixth: The Jewish books in question have never been banned or condemned, either according to ecclesiastical or secular law *(patet per omnia corpora juris et patrum decreta).*

And, therefore, those who argue thusly maintain that said books may not be forcibly confiscated from the Jews, in order to ban or burn them.

In God's Name, so be it, amen.

In order to resolve this question, we must first distinguish the tare from the weed and the chaff from the wheat, so that we do not root up the one with the other, as the Holy Gospel says (Matthew 13:29). So I find that Jewish books are of varying kinds:

First: The Holy Scripture they call *"Essrim varba,"* which means 24; for that is how many books there are in their Bible.

Further: The Talmud, which is a collection of teachings and exegeses based on all the laws and prohibitions in the Torah—that is, in the Five Books of Moses—; 613 in all, which were written down long ago by many of their greatest scholars.

Third: The sublime mystery of the pronouncements and sayings of God, which they call *Kabbalah.*

Fourth: The glosses and commentaries, in particular on the individual books of the Bible, written by various authors and scholars. Such commentaries are called *Perush.*

Fifth: Sermons, disputations and books of sermons, called *Midrash* or *Drashot.*

Sixth: The work of philosophers and scholars of all disciplines; these are commonly called *Sefarim,* which means books, and each is designated according to the discipline of the author.

Lastly: I find poetry, fables, verse, fairy tales, satires and collections of moral examplae. Each of these books has its own name, just as the author conceived it. And these are generally held by most Jews themselves as whimsical works of the imagination.

Among the last mentioned type of books, it may well be that there are several to be found—but very few, I'm sure—which refer somewhat with a certain degree of scorn, using slanderous and blasphemous language to speak of our beloved Lord and God, Jesus Christ, his venerable mother, and also the apostles and the saints. Of such books I have read only two: the one is called *Nizzachon,* the other *Tolduth Jeschu ha-nozri,* the latter of which, moreover, is even considered by the Jews themselves as apocrypha, as Paul von Burgos[1] writes in chapter six of the second half of his "Scrutinium Scripturarum." Indeed, I also remember hearing repeatedly in the course of many conversations with Jews at the court of Emperor Frederick III, of blessed memory, the father of our most merciful Lord, that the Jews themselves saw to it that such books were taken and destroyed and that it was forbidden for their own people ever to express anything of the sort aloud or in print.

But to respond to the question, I would say: If such a book is found among the holdings of a Jew who knowingly harbors it, a book that expressly and clearly heaps scorn, offense and dishonor upon our sacred Lord Jesus, his venerable mother, the saints or the Christian Order, then one would have the right by Imperial mandate to confiscate and burn it and duly punish said Jew for having himself failed to tear it up, burn it or otherwise dispose of it.

Such an action is in my view legally justified, first, based on the article of law that stipulates in *I. Lex cornelia (§. Si quis librum. ff. de iniur.):* "If any person writes, prints or publishes or commissions a book with injurious intent for the express purpose of dishonoring, offending or besmirching the reputation of another, under any of the aforementioned conditions—and even if the book be published under a pseudonym or anonymously, the Court has the right to instruct the local magistrate to bring accusation and to punish the perpetrator."

In addition, another Imperial edict *(I. j. C. de famosis libellis)* states as follows: "If any person discovers a libelous, offensive text, either at home or in a public place or wherever it may be, having no prior knowledge of its existence, he must either tear it up before it falls into anyone else's hands, or at the very least, not tell anyone else about it. If, however, he should not immediately tear up or burn said book, but rather, communicate its contents to another, he must know that he himself will be held liable, and will consequently be condemned and punished. To this should be added, however: If any person comply with this ordinance, either to protect his own interests or for the sake of the common good, let him do so publicly. And let him step forward and stand without fear before the court and explain his reason for presenting such slanderous material to the magistrate. And he should know: If his testimony proves to be true and credible, then he will merit great praise and no small reward from his Majesty. If, however, his testimony does not turn out to be true, then he will forfeit his head. (And even in the case of a credible testimony), the slanderous book in question may not defame another person's good reputation."

From these two rulings of Imperial law we may clearly conclude that a libelous book should be suppressed, confiscated and burned, and whoever fails to do so should be severely punished. And it is all the more justifiable to confiscate such a libelous book from any person who has himself failed to burn and destroy it. Such measures, however, may only be resorted to following a thorough inquest and a legally conducted trial, as the law prescribes: "It is not permissible to confiscate a person's property immediately upon his arrest, but only following the conclusion of a trial in which the verdict has gone against him." So did the Holy Emperor Hadrian ordain in writing *(I. 2. ff. de bo. damnat.).*

So much for the libelous books of the sort referred to in the last part of my listing of the types of Jewish books. In prosecuting the owners of such books, one many not deal any differently with them than one would with any Christian involved in the same sort of affair, since the members of both sects [Judaism and Christianity] belong to the Holy Empire as citizens of the Empire; we Christians being represented by our Lords who elect and empower the Emperor to speak for them, and the Jews belonging through their voluntary and public avowal inherent in the words: "We have no king but

Caesar" (John 19:15). Therefore, the Imperial Law is equally binding for Christians and Jews, each in his own way.

Furthermore, in accordance with His Imperial Majesty's orders, the *Essrim Varba,* that is, the 24 Books of the Bible, shall be excluded from judgment in this recommendation; and rightfully so, for the authenticity of these texts is without question and they are to be held in great honor and preserved (according to St. Jerome and 2 Timothy 3:16). For our Christian religion has taken these same books into its canon *(15. distinctio. c. sancta romana ecclesia),* as proof of the eternal truth, as Magister Sententiarum writes in the preamble to his book.

To begin with, therefore, let me treat the other books, notably the Talmud. This is a collection of the teachings regarding God's commandments, as I have already stated above in the second part of my recommendation. It was compiled, according to written record, some four centuries after the birth of Christ. But I myself have read in Hebrew books that the Talmud is drawn from and comprises the works of many masters and was first assembled into a single cohesive work and issued as a book by Rav Aschi—as is the case for us Christians with the *Decretum [Gratiani]* or *The Book of [the Magister] Sententiarum* or the *Catena aurea*—and this compilation occurred 44 years after the death of Hyrkanos (one of the last Maccabbean high priests). Hyrkanos II, moreover, was the father-in-law of King Herod, and was born in the Christian era. There were, however, others likewise named Hyrkanos, a possible source of confusion in the precise dating of the text. The highborn and most learned gentleman, Count Johan Picus von Mirandel[2] writes in his *Apologia* that the Talmud was compiled a century and a half after the birth of

Christ. There are two versions of the Talmud: the one is called the Jerusalem Talmud and other the Babylonian Talmud.

In any case, it is a fact that the Talmud has existed for far more than a thousand years. The work is divided into four parts, just as we divide our teachings into four higher faculties: Theology, Secular law, Canonical law, and Medicine. The first part deals with sacred matters, holidays and ceremonies; the second with plants and seeds; the third with matrimony and women; the fourth with legal decisions and laws—even though Petrus Nigri[3] divides the Talmud into six parts in his book, *Star of the Messiah,* which was published in Latin and German [in 1475].

Now it may well be that when the teachers of the Jews saw how, following the death of our Lord, the Christians launched a formidable challenge, actively attempting to convert the heathens (as is written in Acts 13), they [the Jews] then called together all their scholars to prevent the demise of the teachings of the old sages, and so as better to counter the heathens and Jews newly converted to Christianity with convincing disputations and rebuttals: for that reason, they collected the decisions and teachings of their fathers and their most famous and learned scholars into a single book. And so that such great effort and work as they and their ancestors undertook in the composition and transcription not be lost, they, therefore, charged their brethren to hold this book (of which God himself must surely approve) forevermore in high esteem. And it is only natural and perfectly reasonable that they should do their best to cite, present, write down and recite everything concerning their laws so that these teachings may not be scorned by their descendants. And all this they did so that they could better defend themselves and hold their own in disputations with the heathens and converted Jews.

Now, alas, to my great regret, I have never myself perused this Talmud, even though I would have gladly paid double the price for the chance to read it. Thus, all my efforts to no avail, I have no direct knowledge of the Talmud itself, but only an indirect knowledge based on our [Christian] books written against it. Still I am willing to believe that the Jews have scattered throughout its pages various and sundry words and sentences directed against our beloved Lord, Jesus Christ, and his friends and followers; just as in his lifetime, they said to his face: that he was nothing but the son of a carpenter and a lowborn woman (Matthew 13:55f.); and that they knew him well, that he was possessed by the devil (John 6:42); and that he was no Jew at all, but a Samaritan and a seducer of the people (John 8:48); that he defames and blasphemes against God (Matthew 26:65); and seeks to declare himself king and to rouse the land and people of the Roman empire to rebellion (Matthew 27:2; 11f.). For this reason, they instigated a trial against him and succeeded in having the imperial judge declare the death sentence against him. One will very likely find in the Talmud sentiments of this sort expressed in passages that bear upon this matter. And since we may find, side by side, in the same chapters many curious references to be used by the scholars as examples in arguments with each other, I am inclined to believe that—were we to have excerpts told or read to us—we might well find it strange and curious stuff indeed.

This I cannot, however, confirm from my own experience, since, lacking a copy, I have not had occasion to consider it. And I know no Christian in all of Germany who has himself actually studied the Talmud. Never, moreover, in my lifetime has there ever been a baptized Jew in the German realm who could either understand or read it (except for the Chief Rabbi of Ulm, who, immediately after being baptized, reportedly converted back to Judaism in Turkey). For although the Talmud is written in Hebrew letters, its language is not pure Hebrew, as we find in the Bible; but rather, we find in its phrasing diverse strains from other Oriental languages, that is, among others, from the Babylonian, Persian, Arabic and Greek. It also contains countless abbreviations, so that a great effort and lengthy study is required of the reader, which is why not many Jews can understand the Talmud, not to speak of Christians.

Thus, I reply to the question at hand that the Talmud must not be burned or otherwise destroyed, for the aforementioned reasons as for the following:

First: It is common knowledge that human reason cannot prevail over superstition and error, which are bound to exist, as Saint Paul writes in the first epistle to the Corinthians, Chapter 11 (19ff.). And this occurs with God's approval, so that the true believers and the saints may rise above the rest, as the Apostle Paul clearly states in the aforementioned passage. And such people are called superstitious who misinterpret the Holy Scripture and willfully adhere to their mistaken belief in direct opposition to the interpretation called for by the spirit of the Holy Ghost. And although the Jews are not, strictly speaking, heretics—for they have never held by the Christian Faith and have, therefore, never left it; for which reason they may also not be called heretics, nor can their practices be labeled heresy—they are, nevertheless, included amongst those referred to by the Apostle, for he speaks of those who are "divided in matters of faith," as are we and the

Jews. For this reason, it is good and useful to us that the Talmud exist and be preserved. And the more full of contradiction the Talmud may be, the more it empowers us Christians to dispute its truth in spoken word and writing.

And if we ourselves are really serious in our spiritual purpose, then preserving the Talmud is good medicine to counteract the indolence and laziness of those who, like the priests, ought to study the Holy Scriptures. It is up to the clergy to instruct themselves and become sufficiently well versed so as to be able, in turn, to pass on the true teachings to others and "by sound doctrine both to exhort and to convince the gainsayers," as St. Paul writes to Titus (Ti 1:9).

Similarly, Aristotle writes in his *Elenchoi* that a wise man should possess two qualities, namely the following: that he not lie, and that he be able to counter that which is the stuff of lies. And he should not fly into a rage and burn the books of his opponents if he has not studied enough to oppose them with reasoned arguments in sermons or disputations. Does dialogue not degenerate into barroom brawl when the crude resort to fists for lack of anything more to say?

It is written in the Psalter (Psalm 141): "Let the righteous smite me; it shall be a kindness: and let him reprove me; it shall be an excellent oil...." Yet how can anyone argue against a thing which he does not understand—as St. Jerome maintains against Jovinian. Thus someone must at least understand the language of the Talmud before asserting that it is false or intentionally offensive to us Christians. For "whosoever knows not the meaning of words and of their language easily errs in his interpretation," says Aristotle in the aforementioned work. And similarly, St. Augustine contends (in *On the True Religion*): "The precise meaning of the Holy Scripture can only be understood according to the unique qualities of each language in which it is written. For each language has its own particular mode of expression which is unique to itself. If this [mode of expression] is taken literally in its translation into another language, it would appear to anyone reading it that the words made no sense at all...." This passage is included in the Canonical Law.

From this we may conclude: Since the Talmud contains the characteristics of so many languages, as noted above, every Jew, even if he is well versed in Hebrew, cannot possibly understand it in its totality. How then can the Christians justify the condemnation of the Talmud, a work which they themselves do not even understand?

Here is an example of what I mean: A pamphlet defaming the Jews has recently been printed;[4] and in it reference is made to a certain prayer included in their [the Jews'] prayer book allegedly to be expressly directed against us Christians. The prayer begins: *"ve-la-meshumadim."* This word is held against them and a great deal is made of it, as if they intended therewith maliciously and scornfully to vilify the Holy Apostles and their baptized successors and the Christian Church in general as well as the Roman Empire. With this, one could easily incite ignorant people unfamiliar with their language to rise up against the Jews, so that they would be in danger of their lives.

If, however, we look closely at this prayer, we find not a single word that either signifies or alludes to the "baptized," or the "Apostles," or "Christians," or the "Roman Empire"! Nowhere in written or spoken form, in this prayer or anywhere else, do we find that *"meshumad"* signifies either "chrism" or "baptism," but rather, its meaning is "to destroy"; as, for instance, in the Book of Proverbs 14:11: "The house of the wicked shall be destroyed"; and in Ezekiel 14:8: "…and I will cut him off from the midst of my people Israel"; and in many other passages. In this prayer, the word *"meshumadim"* is employed as a verb, or more precisely, as a present participle in the active case and signifies: "those who destroy" or "those they destroy," as if they wished to say: Whosoever wants to destroy us, let him harbor no hope that his plot will succeed.

How can this prayer possibly refer to the "Christians," since there is no people on earth that accords them [the Jews] greater freedom and welcomes them more readily than do the Christians, as we may find affirmed in canonical and secular law. And since, by their own attestation, the Jews recognize no other Lord and Master than our Christian Emperor, it is inconceivable that such a prayer would have been composed with the Christians in mind. For they pray it all over the world, wherever they may live—whether among the Turks, under the sovereignty of the Sultan, among the heathens, the Tartars or here in our midst. And indeed, they know all too well that they would be just as unhappy were there no Christians, for they are more hated among the heathens and are more badly treated by them than by us.

Further, *"minim"* signifies "all those who do not adhere to the true faith." How can we presume that this refers to us and to no one else?

Thirdly, *"ʾoyeb"* means "the enemies." That word according to its precise meaning cannot possibly refer to us. For as I have truthfully expounded above, we and they are both fellow subjects in the sole Roman Empire and both enjoy the same rights and privileges and live under the selfsame jurisdiction. How then can we be the "enemies"? A fine gloss to this effect can be found in our law *(in. c. Sicut judaei. super ver. cimiterium ex. de judae).*

Fourthly, *"malchut zedon"* signifies "the dominion of pride" and *"malchut"* does not in itself signify "the kingdom," but would have to be modified to mean "the royal kingdom." This is clearly evident in the Holy Scripture, Joshua 12:7ff.: "And these are the kings of the country which Joshua and the children of Israel smote...." These were not sovereign rulers of royal kingdoms, but rather each was commander of an army loyal to him. And likewise, do we read and sing every day in our churches (Psalm 119:21): "Thou hast rebuked the proud that are cursed...."

So, if not a single word in this prayer signifies precisely "the baptized" or "apostles" or "Christians," or "the Roman Empire"—why then did the law permit such a vile calumny to be printed? And as to those who still suggest that the Jews harbor slanderous intent and secretly referred to us [Christians] in their thoughts—let them remember that no one but the Creator of all hearts can possibly know what any man has in mind. Therefore, no one may rightfully be accused or punished for any such imagined offense *(I. cogitationis. ff. de poen.)*. And even if someone were to step forward and impute his own guilt in this regard, no one else can be held accountable *(I. repeti. §. 1. ff. de quaestio.)*.

I would rather not now take up other words in the same pamphlet which are more than likely not rightly understood and, therefore, not properly translated into German. A single case in point: When they [the Jews] greet a Christian at home or on the street with the words: "Welcome to you!", the author of the aforementioned pamphlet maintains that they are really saying: "Welcome, you...!" meaning: "Welcome, you devil!" This is a grammatical impossibility in proper Hebrew, since *shed* means "devil" only if it has a dot on the right side of the letter *S* (shin); thus it is pronounced "sh": *shed*. Any fool can tell then that *"Sched wilkommen"* sounds nothing like *"Seid wilkommen,"* ("Welcome to you"), since *"shed"* sounds altogether different from *"seid."* Such imputations are nothing but foolish nonsense and childish prattle and do not merit any further attention in this recommendation.

Thus any reasonable person will readily acknowledge and accept the fact that no individual who does not understand the Talmud may rightfully cast aspersion on it (as per canonical law) *(37. distin. in canone Qui de mensa).*

If someone wished to write against the mathematicians and were himself ignorant in simple arithmetic or mathematics, he would be made a laughing stock. So too would be the case of anyone wanting to argue against the philosophers who are unschooled in their methods and teachings. This, according to canonical law.

Hereto someone might, however, object: I do not need to understand the Talmud, since there are so many books in print written against the Jews, books that maintain that the Talmud is evil. And Magister Raimundus[5] writes such foul things about the Talmud in his *Pugio fidei (3. par. dis. 3. c. 20)* that honorable people are inclined to turn away in revulsion. This is likewise true of *Fortalicium fidei*[6] and *Additiones (capituli 34, Isaiae, et Zachariae quinto)* by Paul of Burgos[7] and also *Star of the Messiah* by Brother Petrus Nigri.[8] The same is true of Johannes Pfefferkorn, the plaintiff in this inquiry. They all write that the Talmud is full of scurrilous and reprehensible teachings, and replete with foul language.

To which one might reply: There has never been anyone who in a just and orderly fashion expounded the position of the accused. We have a common saying: Listen to both sides of the story. It is a fundamental principle of law that one may not dismiss as guilty or condemn anyone without first conducting a thorough inquiry and an in-depth investigation into all the circumstances surrounding the case *(23. q. vlt. occidit, et 15. q, vi. c. 1. in fi.).* And even if neither of the parties in a conflict initiates such an inquiry or requests the judge to do so, the latter must, nevertheless, on his own accord, do everything in his power to establish the truth concerning the guilt or innocence of the accused *(I. 2. C. de eden. et ibi glo. et Bart.).*

Therefore, I do not feel bound by what our aforementioned coreligionists have written against the Talmud, being apprised that some of these self-appointed critics have never so much as perused its pages. And so I will not allow myself to be misled by what they have said or written, but will rather in this regard follow the dictates of Canonical Law, which states: "We are not obliged to accept the argument and opinion of every commentator, however piously Christian or well respected he may be, as if it were Holy Writ or established law" *(in ca. Neque quorumlibet distinc. 9).*

For if the Talmud should have been torched, surely it would have been fed to the flames many centuries ago, since our forefathers were far more fervid about their Christian faith than we are today. Never indeed, as far as I can recall, have I read any such suggestion or wish expressed by those who criticize the Talmud—except in the works of the two aforementioned individuals, Brother Petrus Nigri, an ordained priest, and Johannes Pfefferkorn, the recently baptized Jew, both being my contemporaries with whom I have myself already conferred in person. I bear them no ill will, for they have "a zeal for God, but not according to knowledge," as St. Paul says in the Letter to the Romans 10:2.

Whereas the others before us, highly learned and well versed in many languages, did indeed write sharp criticism of the Talmud, yet never did they express the wish that it be burned and destroyed. For them, it is as for a noble hunter, the like of which I have seen among the great lords: The way he hunts a proud stag with a prodigious set of antlers across a wheat field, knowing full well that the beast cannot elude him. And for his own pleasure's sake, the hunter does not want the animal speared or shot down, preferring to see him hunted rather than captured. This is precisely how matters stand for the scholars and other knowledgeable gentlemen who take pleasure in challenging the Talmud and its proponents with reasonable and learned arguments. What glory would be theirs; how would they prove themselves to be reliable scholars and masters of Christian theology if the Talmud had been burned and no longer existed? For in that case, no one could tell any longer if their arguments and refutations were true or false, since the subject of those arguments, the very book they were refuting, was no more!

This is how Saint Paul sees it in the above-mentioned passage (1 Corinthians 11:19): "For there must be also heresies among you, that they which are approved may be made manifest among you." It is for this reason that I maintain: The more preposterous and unfit the Talmud is—as our scholars suggest—the more fervently do I wish it be preserved for our students and theologians, if only as the bull's-eye of their daily intellectual target practice, so that they become all the more ardent and bold in verbal combat with the nonbelievers. For as the soldiers say, "It is best to scale the rampart at its lowest point" *(13. distinc. Nervi).* And if indeed the Talmud were as foolish and evil as some suggest it is, then our people could easily make short shrift of it.

This reminds me of the illustrious warrior, King Agesilaos of Lacedomia, the subject of a lovely little book in Greek by the noble, wise and chivalrous Xenophon (who was himself a fellow student and follower, along with Plato, the very epitome of wisdom, of that most learned Master Socrates). In the book, he tells of the time Agesilaos set out with his army to fight the Persians; the king gave his lieutenants and ensigns the order that whomever of the barbarians they should take captive, they should strip them naked and bring them to the cities and sell them at market. And this was his reason: If his soldiers saw the enemy naked, white and prone from head to toe, they would then think that to fight them would be as easy as fighting wenches, and fortified with such disdain would display all the more their manly courage in combat. Many a formidable leader has since prized this as a remarkably sly tactic and a great piece of wisdom. The fact is, that it served King Agesilaos all the more to let the enemy be sold naked into slavery than to have him slaughtered on the spot; for it kept his troups fit for battle and all the braver on the battlefield.

So much for the first part of my recommendation, founded upon the words of Saint Paul, who says: "For there must be also heresies among you, that they which are approved may be made manifest among you" (1 Corinthians 11:19).

Furthermore, in support of my opinion that the Talmud not be burned, I cite the Holy Gospels themselves. For our Lord Jesus Christ said to the Jews (John 5:39): "Search the scriptures; for in them ye think ye have eternal life: and they are they which testify of me." Since this very passage is the principal pillar of my recommendation, it is right and fitting to begin here by clearly establishing the precise meaning of each word, so as to bypass the many objections of my opponents, should they choose to raise them in this regard.

The first thing the Lord says is: "search." The word in Greek, the language in which the Holy Gospels were first written down, is: *(èreunate)*. And this word has two roots, as our learned scholars of Greek reveal; the one, *(èrō)* or *(èrōtō)* means "to ask" or "seek out"; the second, *(èunē)* means "chamber" or "room for repose," as though it meant a school, *nam schola diciur vacatio* (for *school* means "leisure"). And if then these two roots are combined into a single word: *(èreunō),* then the word must mean "to inquire, to systematically and attentively study and search at leisure." It is as if our Lord Jesus had wanted to say: Deliberate over those writings in your schools in which you fancy finding eternal life, for these books, too, attest to me.

Furthermore, says the Lord in the aforementioned passage: "...for in them ye think ye have eternal life...," and he does not say: "...in which you know for a fact you have eternal life." For the word *(dokei)* ibid. means "to take something for truth which is not true," and so in our common parlance, means "to think" (or suppose). Thus he distinguishes between the books of the Bible on the one hand and the rabbinical commentaries on the other, for he had taught them before that they should know for a fact—and not merely think—that they will find eternal life in the Bible. (Luke 10:26ff.). For among the people, a scholar stood up and said: "Master, what shall I do to inherit eternal life?" To which the Lord replied: "What is written in the law? How readest thou?" To which the latter replied: "Thou shallt love the Lord thy God with all thy heart, and with all thy soul, and with all thy strength, and with all thy mind; and thy neighbor as thyself." And the Lord said: "Thou hast answered right: this do and thou shallt live." Moses had said the very same thing to the Jews long before (Deuteronomy 30:19): "I call heaven and earth to record this day against you, that I have set before you life and death, etcetera." Therefore, they [the Jews] had no doubt that in the Bible they would find eternal life.

At the same time, they had other books that were not a part of the Bible, and which their scholars and rabbis had composed with keen insight. These our Lord Jesus called "traditions" (Matthew 15:1ff.). For this reason, they harbored the false belief that herein too they might find eternal life, and that, of course, was not true. For our Lord Jesus spoke against it and tried to make them understand that they were blind, though they claimed they could see (John 9:41). And so he condemned the books they had written and their life (Matthew 23) in many pronouncements which he directed against the authors of those books and against the priests.

From all this we may conclude that our Lord Jesus was specifically referring in his pronouncements to these books, which comprise the Talmud ("in them ye think ye have eternal life"), when he said: "Search the scriptures in which ye think ye find eternal life, and those...," by which he must mean: these very books as well as the Bible. This is how we must interpret the little words "and" or "also," as if, thereby, he wanted to say: The books compiled by your scribes and scholars, which comprise the Talmud, they too attest to me, as does the Bible.

And this is the truth. For the more the Talmud may be directed against us, the better and stronger are the proofs to be found in it in our favor and that of our Christian Faith. This is the reason why Christ proclaimed that these books should be studied in depth in our schools, that they be debated, and not that they be burned.

I wish only to derive a single argument from the above, an argument able to nip in the bud any objections which the Jews might raise. They say: We gladly believe that Jesus lived, but we do not believe that he is the true Christ (Messiah), for the Christ proclaimed in the Bible has not yet come. If in the Bible, indeed, I find no conclusive proof that he has come, I can prove it to them based on their own Talmud. For their scholars wrote in fact that the law of Moses would become invalid 4,000 years after the creation of the world, and that thereafter, the law of the Messiah will be established and hold sway for the next 2,000 years; for the world would endure for 6,000 years, just as it was created in six days. These are their own predictions, contained in the Talmud, written down and duly transmitted just as they were spoken by the followers of Elijah. Now the Jews reckon the present as the year 5,271, that many years having transpired since the creation of the world; thus they now have 1,300 years left, so that, according to their own reckoning, the true Messiah or Christ must have come 1,300 years ago.

It is, of course, of no concern to me whether or not the sons or followers of the Prophet Elijah actually said this, for my purpose, rather, is to take from their own mouths the proof of what our Christian Faith maintains, which proof they then cannot contradict. Countless references of this sort can be found in the Talmud and used to contradict their position, proof drawn from the very book which they revere and acknowledge.

Now there can be no stronger proof than the testimony of my opponent in a legal proceeding, or the written confession taken from documents or legal instruments readily available for public scrutiny. This we call in the legal profession, *Praesumptio juris* or presumption of law, and this is so highly regarded that no further inquiry into the truth of the matter is required *(tex. et glo. in. I. antiquae. §. sed si quidem. C. ad. S.C. vellei. ubi etiam Bald. in ver tertio quaero utrum ista confessio).*

Now someone might well raise the objection here: Dr. Reuchlin, you have said above that the Talmud was written more than one and a half centuries after the birth of Christ. How, in light of this fact, can it rightfully be claimed that Christ was referring to the scholars of the Talmud when he said: "Search the scriptures, etcetera"? To this I would reply with the words of the most reverend father and learned gentleman, His Grace, Sir Paul, Bishop of Burgos and High Chancellor of Spain, who in the introduction to his book, *Scrutinium scripturarum [Study of the Books]* writes: "Even before the death of our beloved Lord and long before his birth, the scholars and masters of the Jews wrote much and taught and recorded their teachings in various books and documents. But later, once the Christian faith began to grow, long after our dear Lord's death, and in conformity with the explanation of Rabbi Moses of Egypt [Maimonides] in his Deuteronomy *[Mishneh Torah]* (1:13), they held council and systematically compiled all the writings of their scholars and legal authorities into a single work, as it exists today, and called this collection of the teachings of their masters the Talmud." This, at any rate, is what our very own Christian scholars have to say about the matter. And since Christ himself proclaimed that we should draw from it the stuff of our own disputations and proof of his coming, the book must not be burned.

Thirdly: I base my opinion on the tree of the knowledge of good and evil; for God himself planted this very tree in the Garden of Eden (Genesis 2:9). Therefore, it may not be uprooted by any man, an act expressly forbidden by God in Deuteronomy 20:19, where it is written: "…thou shallt not destroy the trees thereof by forcing an axe against them: for thou mayest eat of them." And even though, by tasting of its fruit, Adam and Eve swallowed the seeds of death, God, nevertheless, did not fell the tree or burn it down, but rather left it standing to the present, as we discover daily. And even though some of our fellow Christians maintain that there is much evil in the Talmud, it is surely no evil act to read and study this evil: Not so as to heed the evil, but so that we may better be able to recognize and adhere to the good *(37. distin. qui de mensa).*

And so says Aristotle in his book, *Elenchoi,* that the knowledge of evil is not evil, but rather good and righteous. What good could or might a Moses have been able to learn from the Egyptians, who were themselves devoted to idolatry, and worshiped cats, dogs, snakes and vipers for gods—as Saint Athenagoras, imperial legate and ambassador to Roman emperors Marcus Aurelius Antonius and Lucius Aurelius Commodus, writes regarding his mission to the Christians.

What should Daniel have made of the wisdom of the Chaldeans, under whose yolk he lived (Daniel 1:3f.), a people whose faith was replete with superstitions and spotted with idolatry; of whom it is written (Isaiah 48:20): "Flee ye from the Chaldeans!" And elsewhere, King Solomon is praised, in that his wisdom surpassed that of the Orientals and the Egyptians (1 Kings 4:30). And we have a common saying: "Behold thou art wiser than Daniel" (Ezekiel 28:3). Based on all these references, the canonical law concludes in the aforementioned passages: "The Jewish youths in

Chaldea: Daniel, Ananias, Misael and Azarias, refused to eat or drink at the table of the kings of Babylon, so that their conscience would not be compromised. Had they known that the wisdom and teachings of the Babylonians were a sin for them to study, they would never have willfully learned such things, the nature of which it did not behoove them to know. But they did learn it, not to adhere to it, but rather so as to be able to consider and contradict it." (All of the above, to this point is quoted verbatim from the aforementioned canonical law.)

From this text, we may conclude that it is permissible to read and study good and evil side by side: the evil, so as to effectively combat it with reason; and the good, strewn among the evil like roses among thorns, to be extracted for the sake of our Holy Teachings *(c. turbat. ea. dis.)*.

Now there is no one who can or may in good conscience avow of the Talmud (in which we find the four higher faculties described) that it is altogether evil and that there is no good to be learned from it. For it contains many useful medicinal prescriptions and a knowledge of herbs and roots, as well as many admirable legal decisions compiled by knowledgeable Jews the world over. And in matters of theology, the Talmud offers in many passages a handle to oppose the religious prejudices of the Jews; this is revealed in the books of the Bishop of Burgos concerning the Bible and the commentaries *(Scrutinium),* which he wrote in a Christian and praiseworthy fashion, and in which he plausibly defends our Faith with arguments taken from the Talmud. I have counted more than fifty places in the first part alone of his book, *Scrutinii scripturarum,* in which he employs the Talmud to combat the Jews—not to speak of the second part of the same book, where likewise in many passages, he turns the Talmud to our Christian advantage. And in his introduction, he writes that the glosses and sayings of the Talmud scholars are such that we may derive from them powerful and convincing arguments against the Jews; for regarding hidden sacred truths, their teachers have here and there prophesied and foretold, without being conscious of what they were actually saying, like Caiphas (John 11:49). The testimony of an opponent is very effective proof. This he writes in the aforementioned introduction. And in this same way, he sifts through the entire Bible: And wherever it appears that the Jews are of a different opinion than we, he argues against them in support of our view based on their own Talmud. No one who has read this work can deny its merit.

The other notable scholars of the Holy Scripture do much the same when they wish to argue against the Jews: These learned men, conversant in the Jewish tongue, make reference to the Talmud, and so, combat the Jews with their own book. So, for instance, the renowned theologian, the Doctor of Sacred Letters from the barefoot order of friars, Alfonsus de Spina,[9] who wrote the book *Fortalicium fidei* in Spain, skillfully drew his arguments from the Talmud, particularly in the third book of his study, thus using the Talmud to his and our advantage—as though he wished to stab the Jews with their own knife. This too is the tactic employed by the most learned Dr. Nikolaus de Lyra[10]—a veritable prince of the barefoot order—not only in his analysis of the entire Bible, wherever he may find a useful reference, but also in his own book directed against the Jews, which begins: "We first must ask ourselves if [there is any benefit to be derived] from the books that we have inherited from the Jews, etcetera." And in that work he writes as follows: "Whereas the Talmud and the commentaries of the Jewish scholars do not, for the most part, bespeak the truth, we can nevertheless find there effective arguments to be used against them…"—quoted verbatim. Much the same sentiments have also been expressed by other Christian teachers and theologians, and most notably, by those who left Judaism to become Christians, like the learned professors Petrus Alfonsi[11] and Meister Alfonsus Conversus[12] in his *Libro de bellis dei,* and Meister Johannes de Podico,[13] Meister Hieronymus Conversus, and others.

From all this we may well conclude that the Talmud is no barren tree unable to bring forth good fruit, not a tree to be hewn down and cast into the fire (Matthew 3:10). Rather, it contains much that is good, and learned experts can derive much good from it, as has been shown above—in the spirit of that which St. Jerome writes to Athleta [Laeta, a pious lady in his circle]: "The wise man can find gold in dung."

If, however, the ignorant find cause for annoyance in this, that is their own fault and not the fault of the book! Goats graze on bitter weeds and make sweet milk of it, and from the selfsame flower do honey bees derive their sweet honey and spiders their deadly poison. This is not the fault of the blossom or the flower, but rather the characteristic and nature of those creatures that feed on them. In this same way, there are bad-natured people who misappropriate good words for an evil purpose; and then again, there are good people who can give a felicitous turn to ill-conceived words. And at the same time, of course, there are also many plain and simple folk with no sense whatsoever of lofty thinking; they take and understand their Scripture literally, word for word.

This is precisely what the Emperor Julian did in the books he wrote against us Christians, and wherein he dissects and interprets almost the entire Bible literally, word for word, twisting words with evil intent; and in opposition to which, Saint Cyril wrote several books explaining that a text must not always be interpreted literally word for word. Saint Jerome took up the same problem in an Easter sermon, in which he said: "Can there be anything more scandalous than what we find in the Holy Scripture: That God bid the Holy Prophet Hosea take a whore as his bride; or that Judah had intercourse with his own daughter-in-law, Tamar, and she bore him a child; and that the Holy King David defiled himself in adultery with Bathsheba; and that Onan, son of Judah, spilled his seed on the ground so as to sire no children? If one wished to take these passages altogether literally, then they—and the entire Holy Scripture—would be trashed and scorned by heathens and nonbelievers, like so much excrement and offal"—quoted verbatim. Much follows in the same vein, which anyone can read for themselves. Therefore did [Meister] Freidank[14] rightly say:

> Some we call evil, others good,
> But both may be misunderstood.

All this I maintain, of course, not to vindicate the Talmud in those passages in which it ought to be repudiated; but solely to prove my point that it does not merit being burned or destroyed simply because it contains a few irresponsible and foolish views common to all disputations, particularly when taken literally.

Furthermore, we know for a fact that the sages of old hid their most profound knowledge and wisdom behind the guise of nonsense, dissembled words or allegorical signs; that often enough, they not only made their words incomprehensible but even went so far as to alter the letters. Thus

the Egyptians had two types of script: the one, a common
a-b-c, so that any Egyptian could read it; the other employ-
ing as letters pictographs taken from nature, i.e., beans,
snakes, swords, staffs, branches, eyes, shields and the like.
The latter script (concerning which we still have books written in the Greek language and letters) was only used for sublime sacred mysteries.

Accordingly, it was on this single point that Saint Cyril
based his entire argument against Emperor Julian's satirical
remarks regarding the scapegoat which the Jews loaded
down with their sins each year and chased out into the wilds
(Leviticus 16:10). He replied, namely, that not only the Holy
Scripture but also the ancient sages were accustomed to
expressing the deepest wisdom in a secret language of alle-
gories, metaphors or riddles. From this mode of expression
are derived the six days of The Creation—since all things
were naturally created in an instant; likewise, the double-
edged sword that hangs before paradise; likewise, that God
said he regretted having made man; likewise, that Abraham
saw three men but only addressed one, and the three ate with
him, even though God does not eat; likewise, that God came
down upon Sodom or came up onto Mt. Sinai, since He is
after all omnipresent in his own lofty repose; likewise, that
God should wish to rise up; likewise, that God should live in
this or any other place; likewise, that God be filled with
fierce fury, hatred, anger, vengeance; likewise, that He pos-
sesses a countenance, hands and feet. In the same way, the
old sages call *wisdom* "water" and *ignorance* "hunger and
thirst." We call *physical desire* "harlot," so did Solomon
begin his proverbs with a "harlot" and end with a "virtuous
woman." And in the Holy Gospels, the Kingdom of Heaven
is compared with many things. And Pythagoras, the first

philosopher, calls *justice* "scales," *anger* "fire," *war* "a sword," *error* "an open road," the *gossips* "swallows," as Porphyrius recounts in the first volume of his *History of the Philosophers,* and St. Jerome reminds in his rebuttal to the Priest Rufinus. And precisely so as to grasp Pythagoras' meaning in a few words, Porphyrius forbade his students from promulgating among the common folk the gist of his lectures on matters of higher learning, as Lysis clearly wrote to Hipparch. And the philosophers, thereafter, conscientiously continued to do the same—either by not even permitting their remarks to be written down, or else by insisting that wisdom be alluded to in such veiled language that not everyone could understand it. Plato did likewise, as is apparent in his writings, and particularly in the missives or letters which he addressed to important men. So too did the Druids in France at the time of Emperor Julius Caesar, as he himself reports in his commentaries *(On the Gallic Wars).*

In other disciplines, we find the same, notably in Alchemy, where metals are referred to by the names of the seven planets. This we know from reading *Summa perfectionis magisterii,* by Geber, whom we call the master of masters, and *Rosarium* by Arnold von Villanova, and Lullius' *Codizill,* and the *Libro Vademecum, Libro de Intentione alkimistrarum, Libro Experimentorum,* and the *Rosario* by Magister Johannes Stirus of England, and Arcturus' *Ars,* among many others. In all these books, we find fantastic and curious words and expressions, so we may be inclined to think that they are the ravings of a madman. Yet those schooled in this science know precisely what is meant and that the words are serious and praiseworthy.

The same can be read in the science of medicine, wherein canine feces are called *Album graecum* and dried human flesh *Mumie* etcetera. And ancient poetry—so, too, all of Homer—is full of esoteric knowledge cloaked in wild metaphors and words. This is also the case with Hesiod, Orpheus and Theocritus.

Since all the ancient branches of learning are accorded such freedom and license from time to time to signify something other than the literal meaning of the words, so that the knowledge not fall into the hands of the unschooled and the ignorant—why then should this same freedom be denied the Talmud, to use uncommon words to communicate its secret teachings to its students, so that not every fool can trample it with his unwashed feet and claim to grasp its meaning!

What if now an ignorant fool stepped forward and said: "Oh mightiest Emperor, merciful Lord! His Majesty must suppress and burn the alchemy books, for they are full of slanderous, evil and also mad and ridiculous things written against our Christian Faith. For here, the alchemist is instructed that man should lie under woman until he is sufficiently warmed and fortified to mount her [Reference to the "Chemical Union"]. Seeing as this sort of thing is strictly prohibited under Imperial Law, indeed punishable by death *(I. Cum vir nubit in feminam. C. de adul. et stup.),* and the students of Alchemy learn it *(unde versus. Trude illum sub eam nec fac sui cernere quicquam. Sic crissando laetus erit sub feminae scandens. Cum iacet et pugnat neque tardat sub muliere. Viribus ascendet ipsam sub se cito prendet ec.),* along with countless other senseless commandments and interdictions found in Arcturus' *Ars* and the like, His Majesty would be doing a good deed if he ordered such books to be burned.

And furthermore, what more crazed and foolish a thing could one read than that someone should pretend to be able and instruct his students how to make of the moon (silver) the sun (gold), and of a single moon many suns. And moreover, how to transform a fugitive groom into a faithful mercury, etcetera!

How else would His Majesty reply to such an ox and ass other than to say outright: "You are a lout, more laughable than blameworthy. I can see all too clearly that you have studied nothing of this science. Get out of my sight, I will not burn these books!"

And since such a narrow-minded sot is not capable of grasping the least little inkling of the secrets of a science, and is not even worthy of such knowledge, he will inevitably misinterpret what he reads—would His Majesty conclude that such books ought to be burned, just because an uneducated reader might not be able to grasp their true meaning? I am quite convinced, your answer would be: No.

Have not the books of the ancient poets been preserved, though they contain much more scandalous things than are to be found in the Talmud, and stand in much greater contrast to our Christian Faith than does the Talmud! Furthermore, all philosophy derives from Homer, the first poet, even though in his false tales he spared neither God nor the world. It was Homer's works, after all, that Alexander the Great assiduously studied by day and placed under his pillow at night, as the fountain of all human and sacred wisdom! Likewise did Saint Chrysostomos read daily from the poet Aristophanes and hold him in high esteem as a model for his stylus, shaping and sharpening all his sermons, which he published in countless volumes, based on Aristophanes' example—even though the former was a pagan poet and a fabricator of lies. Therefore, the canonical law says *(dis. 37. in canone Legimus)*: "We read certain things so that their wisdom not lie fallow; other things we read so to take cognizance of them; and finally, there are some things we read, not to accept what is said, but rather to repudiate it." In this regard, Saint Basilius, likewise, wrote his own tractatus, insisting that we should and could read all books, so that they may be of service—precisely in the aforementioned way.

Among all these learned and pious men, the defenders of our Christian Faith, there is not a one who ever desired or wished that such books as those referred to above be burned or suppressed. Hereby, do we but follow the dictates of our beloved Lord Jesus Christ, as He instructed in Matthew 13:29f.: That we should not uproot tares with weed, lest we destroy the good fruit, but we should rather let both grow together until the harvest. And He explains, thereafter, just when this harvest is to take place: "The harvest is the end of the world." Then will the householder, that is, God himself, say unto the reapers: "Gather ye together first the tares, and bind them in a bundle to burn them." Bear in mind that even then, God does not wish to burn down the entire field for the sake of the tares and weed, but rather, He wishes that the weed alone be selected out and bound into sheaths, and that this faggot or bunch be burned. Thus the Holy Christian Church, faithful to these dictates, rules in its canonical law (in *ca. Sancta romana ecclesia 15. distinc.*), that all books must be preserved so that they may be winnowed and studied, according to the words of the Apostle Paul (1 Thessalonians 5:21): "Prove all things; hold fast that which is good."

But if we burn them, then our descendants will not be able to sift through them for that which is good. For this same reason, the Holy Church decrees that the books of Rufinus[15] and Origen[16] should be preserved, with the exception of those passages and chapters repudiated by Saint Jerome, etcetera. This we may, no doubt, interpret to mean that our mother, the Holy Christian Church, forbids us to burn any book in which there is some bad mixed in with what is mostly good. It is also true, however, that if a book were found to be altogether bad and from which no good might be derived—were it in our power and our jurisdiction, then we would rightfully and lawfully be authorized to destroy and burn it. I am thinking, for instance, of the books of certain heretics, who, because they broke away from our common Christian Faith, were repudiated by the authorities and councils of the Church. If they wrote or issued any statements concerning matters of faith that contradicted the statutes and decrees of the Holy Council and the highest authorities of Christendom, then by judgment or legal decree, such a work could rightfully be destroyed. This was precisely the case in matters concerning the condemned and damned heretic by the name of Eutyches,[17] or of Nestorius[18] and their respective followers, who at the Councils of Chalcedony and Ephesus (Canon 5) were condemned to be excommunicated and executed. At that time, the Roman Emperor as executive head and executor of the assemblies and councils of the Christian Church, decreed that such heretical books as those that stood in opposition to the Chalcedonian and Ephesian Councils be burned *(I. quicumque. §. Nulli etiam et .I. damnato. C. de haeret. et manich.).*

This decision, however, is based on an altogether different set of circumstances and legal proceedings in no way comparable to the case in question. For heretics, precisely because of their having been baptized and their acceptance of the other sacraments, are bound to comply with the Christian Church and are, therefore, in matters of faith, subject to the judgment of no one but the Pope and the priests of our faith

(c. ut inquisitionis. §. prohibemus de haeret. 1L. 6). The
Jews, on the other hand, in matters concerning their faith,
must answer to none but their own judges. No Christian can
or may pass judgment on their spiritual affairs, except in connection with a secular trial initiated by a proper accusation
brought before an established court of law *(I. judaei et ibi
Bart. C. de judaeis).* For they [the Jews] do not belong to the
Christian Church and, consequently, their faith is of no concern to us *(glo. paenul. in cle. 1. de usur.).* Consider the
words of Saint Paul (1 Corinthians 5:12f.), where he says:
"For what have I to do to judge them also that are without?
Do not ye judge them that are within? But them that are without God judgeth!"—quoted verbatim.

And so, concerning the Talmud, I say: Let it neither be
suppressed nor burned.

Now I come to the third category in my classification
of Jewish books: those treating the sublime mystery of the
pronouncements and words of God, known as the Kabbalah.
I could easily say a great deal on the subject—both for and
against it. For twenty years ago, our most Holy Father, Pope
Innocent VIII, ordered this material, namely the books of
the Kabbalah, to be studied and appraised by many very
learned bishops and professors; this in response to the challenge of that most noble and learned gentleman, Count
Johann Pico della Mirandola, of blessed memory, who at the
time called for a scholarly disputation in Rome, and posted
notices announcing the event. Among other themes and the-
ses for deliberation, he also presented the following: "There
is no body of learning that offers more conclusive evidence
of the Godhead of Christ than magic and the Kabbalah."
Our exegetes of the Holy Scripture spoke and wrote a great
deal, however, to prove the contrary, even though they had

no in-depth notion of just what sort of beast this "Kabbalah" might be. With great conviction, nevertheless, the Count overturned their arguments. Whereupon, Dr. Peter Garcia, Bishop of Barcelona, countered with a further written attack against the Count, which he dedicated to Pope Innocent. And finally, following Innocent's death, Alexander VI became Pope. He, in turn, ordered many highly learned cardinals, bishops and Magister Palatii to thoroughly look into the matter and advise him regarding the positions for and against presented in the writings and speeches of both of the aforementioned parties. Thus did His Holiness conclude, thanks to their efforts, that the aforementioned Count Johann did rightfully study the books of the Kabbalah and that his books on the subject are well founded. Subsequently, in the year 1493, he therefore, issued a papal letter in which he approved of the Count's book on the subject, entitled *Apologia*. In that work, Count Pico conducts a thorough study of the Kabbalah and concludes that these books, of which there are some seventy, reveal not only the spiritual heritage of the holy man, Moses, but also offer a substantiation of the truth of our Christian Faith. He maintains, furthermore, that Pope Sixtus IV had ordered that these very books of the Kabbalah be translated into Latin and thus made accessible for study, since they would be of particular importance for our Christian Faith. Of said books, only three have been issued to date in Latin.

On the basis of all of the above, and also because I myself have read many of the books of the Kabbalah, I could, in connection with this recommendation, dwell at length on the pros and cons of the argument. Since, however, one can conclude with certainty from the book, *Apologia,* by the aforementioned Count della Mirandola (approved by Pope Alexander) that the

books of the Kabbalah are not only harmless, but also emi-
nently useful for our Christian Faith; and since Pope Sixtus IV
ordered that they be translated into Latin for the benefit of us
Christians, it will suffice for me to draw the conclusion therefrom concerning said kabbalistic books, that neither should
they nor may they lawfully be suppressed or burned. So that,
however, this part of my argument be likewise substantiated,
let me refer back to the [apocryphal] third book of Ezra of our
Bible, where in chapter 9, we read of the 70 books inspired by
God, not intended to be understood by every man.

Further: As to the fourth category in my classification
of Jewish books, the commentaries and glosses on the Bible,
I recommend that they neither should nor may lawfully be
suppressed or burned, for the following reason:

They explain precisely how every word of the Bible is
to be understood in the particularity of its linguistic context—as we find, for instance, in the work of Abraham ben
Ezra, Moses ben Gabirol and Rabbi David Kimchi, all of
whom offer a grammatical analysis of each word. We should
be no more inclined to burn these books than we would be to
burn such Latin grammars as *Das Fuellhorn,* or those written
by Priscianus,[19] Servius[20] and Donatus[21]—all pivotal texts in
our understanding of Latin. The same holds true for the commentaries and textual glosses of Rabbi Solomon [better
known as Rashi],[22] Rabbi Moses of Garona,[23] Rabbi Levi ben
Gershon—known as Magister Leo de Banolis,[24] the two
learned masters, father and son, Rabbi Joseph[25] and Rabbi
David Kimchi,[26] the latter's brother, Moses Kimchi[27] and
many others who painstakingly elucidate the Old Testament,
word for word, according to the particularities of the Hebrew
language; just as Eustathius [twelfth-century archbishop,

rhetorician] did for Homer, and Theon [Greek astrologer] for Ptolemy and other commentators have done.

I also maintain, and have my sources to back me up, that if our clerics and exegetes of the Holy Scripture truly wish to win out in their debates with those of divergent faith, they had best familiarize themselves with such commentaries, glosses and explications to gain a complete understanding of the Biblical text. For according to sacred canonical law *(c. ut veterum librorum dis. 9),* the religious significance of the books of the Old Testament can only be established through a careful reading of the original Hebrew text. And if, for instance, all the definitions and glosses of Rabbi Solomon [Rashi], who wrote about the Bible, were to be stricken from the books of Nikolaus de Lyra,[28] who also wrote about the Bible, then I could well sum up what's left, namely Nikolaus de Lyra's original contributions to Biblical research, in a few short pages.

The Christian Church can and may not cast aside such commentaries, for they keep alive the original Hebrew, a vital element which the Holy Scripture, and in particular the Old Testament, cannot do without; just as we can and dare not do without the Greek language and its grammars and commentaries for our understanding of the New Testament, as the aforementioned statute of canonical law, *Ut veterum,* clearly states. In this regard, I take the liberty to point out, with all due respect, that one can find a good many scholars in Christendom who because of their ignorance of these two languages [Hebrew and Greek], cannot rightly explicate the Holy Scripture, and in this are often made a laughing stock. Therefore, we should by no means suppress the commentaries and glosses of those who have thoroughly mastered their mother tongue, having studied it since their youth, but rather, wherever such commentaries exist, we should make them accessible, take pains to preserve them and hold them in high esteem as sources from which we may derive the true meaning of the language and the significance of the Holy Scripture. Consequently, the canonical law prescribes *(in ca. jejunium 76. distinc.):* "Many of our scholars have frequently contradicted each other. It is, therefore, necessary and imperative that we turn to the Jews and seek out the truth at its source, rather than its trickle"—quoted verbatim.

Someone might well object: I will gladly make do with our own commentaries, but why do I need the commentaries of the Jews? Here too, I have a ready reply: Whoever is obliged to "make do" is at a distinct disadvantage—like a man in winter with nothing to wear but pants. If we consider, furthermore, that our commentators often enough make so bold as to attempt to explicate books that they themselves have not rightly understood, then no friend of the truth can content himself with the result. The illustrious teacher St. Hilarius wrote glosses and commentaries on the Holy Scripture which are lauded and accepted by the entire Christian Church. Often enough, however, he was badly mistaken in his understanding of individual words, for lack of Hebrew, a language he did not know. And as to his Greek, suffice it to say that his knowledge was breezy at best, as St. Jerome writes in his letter to Marcella concerning the 126th Psalm, and in his letter to Damascus concerning *Hosanna,* and also in many other passages enumerated and verifiable in my book, *De Rudimentis hebraicis.*

Further: Let us consider their books of sermons and disputations, and also their breviaries, hymnals and the compilations of their rituals, customs and devotional prayers. What else should I say of them than that which has already been said and so passed into law, in the secular realm, by our praiseworthy emperors, and in the religious realm, by the popes? "That they [the Jews] are to be left in peace in their synagogues, ceremonies, rites, habits, customs, and devotional prayers, particularly if they do us no harm and display no public disrespect for our Christian Church. For the Christian Church has nothing whatsoever to do with them, other than in the nine points cited in the legal gloss" *(c. judaei ex. de judaeis).*

It is, therefore, my opinion that books of the aforementioned kind should not be confiscated, destroyed or burned *(c. Consuluit ex. de judaeis et. I judaeos. C. eo. ti),* unless they prove to be libelous or concern the "forbidden arts."

Finally, let us consider the books that treat philosophy, the humane and natural sciences and other related areas that comprise the sixth category of my classification of Jewish books. Of these, let me say that I believe they should be treated precisely the same way their Greek, Latin or German counterparts are treated: Teachings and practices which are not forbidden should not be meddled with. If however, Jewish books were brought forward that taught or offered instruction in the "forbidden arts," such as magic, devil worship or witchcraft, and if said books sought to inflict harm on people, one would then be justified in tearing up, or burning, or otherwise disposing of them as anathema to human nature *(I. ceterae. ff. famil. hercis.).* In the event, however, that such books of magic contain only that which is good and beneficial to human life and nothing injurious, then one should not burn or otherwise dispose of them *(tenet Azo. in summa. C. de malefi. et mathemat. circa fi. fa. 1. eorum. C. eo. ti. et in Bart.),* except for those books about grave robbery *(I. 1. C. de thesaur. li. 10).*

Herewith, your Lordship, you have my answer to the question posed by His Imperial Majesty: In sum, it seems to me to be neither praiseworthy to God, nor useful to our Holy Christian Faith, nor conducive to the growth of Godly worship to forcibly seize, suppress or burn the Jews' books— with the exception of slanderous works, which we may designate as *libelli famosi,* and books of the "forbidden arts," which are injurious to all men and, therefore, not to be tolerated, as I have already explained above. For the Jews are, in a certain sense, our Capsarii, cataloguers and librarians, who preserve for us those books from which we may derive proof of our Christian Faith, as the Church Father St. Thomas says in his Summa *(ad Romanos capitulo 9, lect. 2. super verbo: Mailor serviet minori).*

It seems to me, furthermore, in the face of such reasoning, that the counterarguments and justifications of my opponents, which I enumerated at the beginning, fall flat, namely that:

First: The Jews wrote their books to oppose the Christians—an argument, moreover, with no bearing on those books written before the birth of Christ, as I have already noted, or books written for other disciplines. And even if they had written all their books to oppose us, then for that very reason, they should not be burned. For the Jews wrote their books in their own interest to defend their faith, whenever they were attacked, be it by heathen, Tartar, Turk or Christian—and certainly not to malign, slander or injure anyone.

Their innocence in this regard is also to be assumed, since they live as a tiny minority in our midst and are more inclined to serve than to injure anyone. So says the canonical law *(23. q. ult. c. dispar.).* Thus, it should neither be assumed nor imputed that they wrote these books against us, but rather for their own sake. And it may very well be that I happen to do something in my own interest that you may find offensive to you and yours—and yet if I do not expressly intend to injure you, then you have no right to bring suit against me for libel *(I. 1. §. Denique. Marcellus. ff. de aqua. plu. arc.).*

Let us assume for the moment, however, that the Jews had, in fact, written their books with the deliberate intent to oppose us—a premise which I am not seriously suggesting and which would require convincing proof to substantiate—even then, one might well advance as a legitimate excuse that they did so, not to offend anyone, but rather only in their own self-defense. For after having to endure, year after year, the public calumny we heap upon them in our churches on Good Friday, calling them: *"perfidos judaeos,"* that is "faithless Jews," or in good German: "those neither faithful nor true to their faith," they might rightfully reply among themselves: "They slander us. We have never disavowed our faith" *(iux. determinata Panor. in c. Cum te ex. de sen. et re judi. 9. col. ibi. Ego vero distinguo).*

And that which they might be inclined to say, they could elaborate upon and put all the more clearly in writing, so as to exonerate themselves amongst their own people; as Aristotle writes in *Peri hermenias:* "The written word is a facsimile of the spoken word." Therefore, it is simply wrong to suggest that the Jewish books should be burnt because they were written to oppose us. We know that the Christian Church would not have us burn other books with revolting titles, books which are expressly directed against us with the intent to knock us down, such as the writings of Porphyrius, Celus, Julianus Apostata and others.

Now to the second argument, according to which it is maintained that such books slander Jesus, Maria and the Apostles, as well as us and our Christian Order.

This argument and the underlying fact would indeed be convincing, for which reason such texts, wherever they may be found, head off the list of those I have already repudiated. I have never, however, either seen or read anything of the kind, save two books: namely, *Nizzachon* and *Tolduth Jeshu ha nozri*. In all other books which I have until now had occasion to peruse or read, I find no such slander. For as to matters of faith, they [the Jews] are of the opinion that their faith is true and ours is untrue.

Indeed, certain Jews hold the view that every nation ought to be allowed to practice its own faith; and just as we are not bound by the Laws of Moses, so they are not subject to the Laws of Jesus; rather, they are bound to comply with Moses' Laws, for God gave them to the Jews and to no one else. And we are, likewise, obliged to adhere to Jesus' Laws, for God gave them to us. Therefore, everything that they [the Jews] write serves to demonstrate that Jesus is not God; and consequently, all that follows therefrom is a matter of their faith, by which they mean to malign no one. And this the Christian Church has accepted and tolerated for some 1400 years now and never taken any offense in it *(c. consuluit in fi. ex. de judae)*. Jesus appeared on this earth in the form of a man and a servant, as St. Paul writes to the Philippians (2:5f.). As a man and nothing else, this is what the Jews have always held Him to be, seeing nothing sacred in Him, his mother, or in the Apostles—which is what they maintain to this day. I leave it to the good judgment of those who dealt with the aforementioned issues in the secular law *I. Item apud .§. Si quis virgines. ff. de iniur.* and canonical law *c. in audientia ex. de sent. ex.* to decide whether this constitutes an offense.

Now to the third argument: that the books are false. This charge I cannot rightly comprehend, since the term *false* has various meanings, depending on the context.

First off, we sometimes adjudge those books false that have not been properly corrected, in which, for instance, a word has been left out or added, or the letters have been faultily transcribed. This failing merits no special punishment other than to insist that such books be properly corrected and, so, improved, if they are to be rightly understood. For if the books in question should be burned simply because they were inaccurately written down and transcribed, then we would have to burn many copies of the Holy Bible. And whoever is not inclined to accept my contention in this matter need only read St. Jerome's second introduction to the Books of the Chronicles *(AT, Paralipomena),* his introduction to the Book of Job and his other writings, in particular, his epistle to Lucinius Beticus, in which he says that some scribes make more mistakes than others. St. Augustine says much the same in a missive or epistle to St. Jerome *(in. 1.pte Hieronymi epi. c. 6).* And if then we were to burn those books that are false in this regard, i.e., faultily transcribed or printed, then we would have to begin by burning Pliny's useful *In Naturali Historia,* since for centuries there has never been a single correct copy of this work, but only faulty editions. Then, too, did the first scribe to record the Holy Gospel According to St. Matthew err and make mistakes in his transcription, as St. Jerome points out in his letter to Hedibia?

Secondly, we also sometimes call a thing false that is not true, as the word is commonly employed by the philosophers; and in the language of the law, *falsa causa, falsa demonstratio, falsa grammatica, falsa relatio, falsa denoia-tio* and the like are not punishable *(dan. I. Corne),* entailing no deception, and are not considered lies *(I. quid sit falsum in fi. ff. ad I. cor. de fal.).* And even in the case of a legal plea, it is not punishable to waver from the truth; punishment holds only for perjury in the case of a witness's testimony *(sic Bal. in .I. quicumque vlt. col. C. de ser. fugi.).* And if in this regard, the Jewish books may appear to be false, according to our way of thinking, they are, nevertheless, not false according to their [the Jews'] own way of thinking, and according to their faith *(fa. I. in synagoga. C. de judae.).* Consider the law that forbids any person who wishes to act against the Jews from doing so in their house of worship; the gloss states specifically in regard to the term *"domus reli-gionum" (s. judaeorum. q. ad eorum opinionem religiosa)* that they [the Jews] themselves hold it to be sacred and a place of worship.

Thirdly, a thing is called false which, with malice aforethought, suppresses or falsifies the truth so as to harm another *(In auten. de instru. caut. col. 6. circa prin. junc. I. Nec xemplum. C. ad. I. corne. de fal.).* Well then, I know of no people on this earth that takes greater pains to faithfully transcribe the Holy Scripture than do the Jews. For they have organized the Bible in such a way as to prescribe precisely how many verses or coda (which they call *"Psukim"*) comprise each book. Furthermore, they indicate just how often a certain word appears in their Bible. And furthermore, their Bibles, which are printed in numbered verses, contain *"Massoreth"*: these are scholia [footnotes] that indicate the appearance of an [Hebrew] alphabet letter too many or too few. I have never read or heard tell of such a thing in any other language. It is indeed true, we must admit, that a few inconsequential changes can be found in their Bible, which they insist are corrections made by Ezra and Nehemiah, and of these there are some 16 cases. For instance, in Genesis 18:22, it is written: "but Abraham stood yet before the Lord," where before the time of Ezra and Nehemiah it allegedly read, "and the Lord stood before the Lord"; and in Habakkuk 1:12, "O Lord my God, Mine Holy One, we shall not die," where formerly it read, "Mine Holy One, and you will not die," etcetera. Such changes were not made to deceive anyone, for they [the Jews] have themselves noted wherever changes were made. And St. Jerome, as well as the 72 translators [of the Septuagint] transferred those changes into the Latin and the Greek a good thousand years ago. I can find no other reason to impute and prove that they [the Jews] falsified their books.

For the Biblical text is identical in the Orient and the Occident—with the sole exception of that which is argued by their grammarians concerning individual words (something like our *Castigationes* by Hermolaos Barbaros concerning Pliny). That sort of thing, however, is nothing more than the stuff of disputation and scholarly exercise.

The misapprehension, however, on the part of some of our scholars who believe that the Jews falsified their Bible, may derive from the fact that there are many Bible translations in existence: (1) the Chaldean translation of Onkelos and Jonathan; (2) the Greek translation of the 72 translators (Septuagint); (3) the translation by Aquila; (4) the translation by Symmachus; (5) the translation by Theodotion; (6) the translation by Origines in his work, *Hexapla;* (7) the Vulgate; (8) the translation by "Anonymous"; (9) the untitled translation by an unknown scholar. All of these were already available to St. Jerome when he set out to translate the Bible a tenth time—into Latin. An account of this can be found in his commentary. But the immaculate original Jewish text predates all these translations. It would come as no surprise if so many translations and transmissions gave rise to marked changes and distortions, in short, to a falsification of the sort we do indeed find and of which the aforementioned St. Jerome writes (on Ezekiel 40:5, concerning the verse: "And behold a wall on the outside of the house round about…"). He clearly establishes here that "in the Latin and Greek translations, almost all Hebrew words and names are antiquated, distorted and transposed by the foolish and semi-illiterate clerics who transcribed them. And if such an untutored scribe copies from a faulty text, it must necessarily follow that the Hebrew words are turned on their heads and come out as Persian, Bohemian, Hungarian or gibberish. For just because a word may cease to be Hebrew, it does not necessarily follow that it be transformed into a recognizable word in some other tongue"—quoted verbatim.

In the case of all such questionable passages in the Old Testament, we are instructed by canonical law *(9. dis. c. ut veterum),* to refer back to the original Jewish texts. This is convincing proof that the Christian Church still considers them to be the most dependable source, and so not false.

If, however, one were to impute that the Jewish scholars falsely interpreted their books, one could just as well counter that, since we depend on these very interpretations in support of our own faith, citing and applying them to bolster our position (as I have already mentioned), in so doing, we employ false witness, which is after all against the law *(I. si falsos. C. eo. ti.).* But whatever the case may be, a scholar who interprets the Scripture to the best of his abilities, as he sees fit, the result being conclusive or not, in so doing is committing no fraud (unless he knowingly draws upon a falsified text [*I. fi. ff. de fal.*]). Otherwise, all that can be said is that he is mistaken. For it is common knowledge that no one is compelled to accept the views or writings of any one scholar: Thus, no scholar can be accused of deceiving anyone *(I. in .I. in glo. mag. C. de leg.).*

Consequently, this is my response to the aforementioned allegation of falsity: Even if one could find anything false or untrue or fraudulent in the Jews' books, that would not be reason enough, in the eyes of the law, to burn such books *(Ad hoc allego Bart. in .I. quid sit falsum. ff. de fal. ubi dicit: non puto, quod pro quolibet dolo et qualibet deceptione quis incidat in falsum, ut puniatur. I. cornelia de fal., nisi sit de capitulis expressis in hoc titulo.—haec ille.). Hereto, I refer to Bartolus.*[29]

Now to the fourth argument: That having been brought up on their books since childhood, the Jews are, thereby, induced to stubbornly adhere to their Jewish faith and are all the less inclined to become Christians.

It may be true what they say: That what you learn in youth stays with you till old age. "It is so important to acquire good habits in youth," says Virgil (*Georgics* 2, v. 272), and Horace writes in the Second Epistle to Maximus Lollius: "A pot will long retain the taste of that which was first cooked in it." This premise, however, often enough proves false; many times indeed we find that people inept in their youth become most dexterous adults, far surpassing others, as Valerius Maximus[30] writes *(li. vi. ca. 9).*

But let us now set aside the Romans and consider the Jews themselves. Our Apostle Paul was schooled in all Jewish wisdom and studied with the rabbis. And what became of him? The greatest of all apostles! One might well say: It was

God who reared him. To which Christ replies (John 6:65): "No man can come unto me, except it were given unto him of my Father." This then is no valid objection; for all of us who come to the Christian faith are reared into it. "We are not born Christians, but are rather made Christians," says St. Jerome in his epistle to Athleta *(Laeta)* concerning the education of her daughter. For Christ's word comes into the ears, and through the ears into the heart, and from the heart into the will, and through the will it crystallizes into conviction—and from this derives faith. Therefore, says St. Paul in his Epistle to the Romans (10:17): "So then faith cometh by hearing, and hearing by the word of God." From this I may well conclude the following: He who is inclined to hear is inclined to believe, and he who is disinclined to hear is likewise disinclined to believe. Yet a person previously practiced in learning that reveals the subtleties of faith to the faculty of reason is far more likely to heed the Christian credo, for as Aristotle says in *De Anima:* "The effect on a thing is stronger if that thing is primed to receive it."

So if I am to make a position plausible to a sensible person, then I must present it to his reasoning faculty in such a way that his reason not be repelled, so that in the course of critical reflection his free will may lean to this side, and not to that. And if a matter is elucidated in this manner, then free will readily accords with reason and results in faith.

These are the means by which human reason may glimpse a glimmering of truth, as our most learned scholars of the Holy Scripture have written: in the portentous words of the Prophets; the accordance of prophecy and fulfillment in the written text; the supreme perfection of the Holy Books; their accomplished rational way of presenting a thing so that the very supposition of its opposite runs contrary to

reason; the lack of logic apparent in all heterodoxy; the staying power of the Christian Church and the manifest occur-
rence of conspicuous miracles. By these means, the free will
of an unbeliever can be guided and he can be made to see
reason and to believe a thing he previously doubted. It is evident, therefore, that a learned Jew can more easily be converted with a valid argument than can an unschooled Jew. I
stress "with a valid argument," and so do not speak of those
who came to us as a consequence of jealousy, hatred, fear of
punishment, poverty, protection against acts of vengeance,
ambition, for worldly pleasure, sheer gullibility and the like:
Those who would become Christians by word and in name
alone. I have known many such converts, and nothing good
has come of them. This sort is inclined to believe one thing
just as well as another; and if they don't get what they want
in our camp, they run off to Turkey and go back to being
Jews. Let us not speak of such rascals here, but rather of
those valiant, upright Jews and Jewesses, who recognize the
error of their ways, and fully fathom wherein and to what
extent they are wrong, and for the sake of God and truth can
be won over to our Christian faith.

Therefore, I maintain in reply to the fourth argument
cited above: The books, in truth, are not the reason why the
Jews do not come over to the Christian faith (Luke 16:29:
"They have Moses and the prophets"). But rather, the books
might well be the reason they could easily be won over to the
Christian faith, if indeed we had capable enough people who
knew their [the Jews'] language and knew how to hold their
own with them in levelheaded debate. I substantiate my claim
based on the story and the fact which the author of *Fortalicium
fidei*[31] recounts in Book Three, Observation 21 of that work, in
which he writes that one of the most learned and wisest Jews

came to him and spoke much with him concerning matters of faith, and said to him: "that he truly believed in the Christian Faith; to which conviction he was brought by diligent study of the Scriptures, not only the Bible, but also the Talmud and philosophical works"—quoted verbatim. In the same way were Dr. Petrus Alfonsus, Dr. Alfonsus de Spina, Dr. Johannes de Podico, Dr. Hieronymus the Convert, Dr. Paul de Burgos all converted, individuals who seem to me to be more valuable for the cause of our Christian faith than 400 Jewish illuminators or money lenders.

Let us suppose, however, that the Talmud were the reason that they do not become Christians—that is no justification for taking and burning anyone's possessions, for we, as mere mortals, have no right to pass judgment on them. The Jew is as worthy in the eyes of our Lord God as am I. If he stands upright, he stands before his Lord. If he falls, he falls before his Lord. Every individual will have to answer for himself. How can we pass judgment on the soul of another? God is surely mighty enough to lift him up. St. Paul says it all very clearly in Romans 14:4. We also know from the Gospels that our Lord harshly rebuked his disciples Jacob and John for wanting to call heavenly flames down upon a city of unbelievers, who refused to receive Christ and his followers (Luke 9:53ff.). From this, I conclude that the powers that be are blameless in this regard: For they do not acquiesce to evil, but rather merely let it be *(dicto. c. Consuluit Judaeis, et Augustinus de Ancona in libro de ecclesiastica potestate. q. 24. §. ad secundum),* and cannot prevent it, lest they do injustice to innocent people, which they may not do.

To conclude, in the matter of this dispute: I can truly not conceive how anything good can come to our Christian faith [from such a rash act] or how it can promote the veneration of God. I can, however, well imagine how much bad we would do by burning their books.

First: The Jews may claim we are taking their weapons away from them and that we are afraid of them, that they can outdebate us and are wiser than we. It is as if a duke were to challenge a shepherd to a duel, but beforehand, had the shepherd's staff, sword or knife taken from him, while he himself kept his!

Further: The Jews might well write much stranger stuff from scratch, far more objectionable than these books, and a hundred years from now they could tell their children whatever they please about the contents of the burnt books.

Third: They might likewise later assert that our scholars had falsely quoted from theirs and misconstrued their meaning. We would have nothing then to bring as proof in support of our position.

Fourth: Forbidden fruit is all the more desirable. For that reason, their rabbis and scholars would simply go to study in Turkey, and thereafter, following their return, be all the more zealous in their teachings and perhaps tell their children worse things than they learned before.

Fifth: It might well come to pass, as the world keeps changing from year to year, that we urgently need such books at future Church councils and gatherings: Just as the Council of Basel sought to consider the Koran, Mohammed's book, which then Cardinal Johannes von Ragusa brought forward—we would then have to pay dearly for having burnt the books. This is just what happened to the Romans, after King Tarquinius Priscus had the books of the Sybil Amalthea burned, all except for the last three; for which he then had to pay a full three hundred gilders in gold, very much regretting that he had had the other books burned.

Sixth: We are forbidden to enter into public debate with heretics who have fallen away from our faith *(I. dannato et .I. quicumque C. de haeret.)*. With the Jews, however, we may well debate and converse, so as to win them over to our faith *(c. quam sit laudabile et ibi glo. 1. ex de iudae. iuncto. 23. q. 4. c. infideles)*. Yet if their books had been burned— on what sources would we base our challenge other than the text of the Bible? But the latter would count for nought, since the canonical law states *(37. dis. c. relatum)* that there are many words in the text of the Holy Scripture whose meaning can be stretched in such a way as to suit anyone's interpretation. And therefore, the wise Jews would think up interpretations other than those they learned from their fore-fathers, and we would consequently be forced to bow out of any future debates.

Seventh: If there were no more outsiders—whether Jews or heathens—with whom we could wrestle over the meaning of the Holy Scripture, then we ourselves would clash with each other in our scholarly interpretations—for the mind never rests. We would invent newfangled notions, or reawaken old disputes—just as has recently occurred concerning the conception of Our Beloved Lady, or over whether St. Paul was married, or if St. Augustine was a monk and other nonsense. And this sort of thing occurs when we have no one who dares to contradict us, with whom we can lock horns. Consider what the Roman histori-ans write concerning the third war against the City of

Carthage: In the course of deliberation in the Roman Senate on the fate of Carthage, Cato the Censor was of the opinion that Carthage ought to be razed to the ground. Whereupon, Scipio Nasica advised: "No, let us leave Carthage intact." Not for love of that city—for he was just as hostile to it as the others—but rather, for the sole reason that he knew the Romans well enough to fathom that they could not remain inactive for long. And if they had no war to wage outside their realm, then they would start a civil war in their own city and set upon each other, as did indeed happen—and all Rome would have rejoiced in retrospect had they followed Scipio's advice.

Eighth: There is nothing to be gained from burning Jewish books in Germany, where the smallest number of Jews reside. For they still have other schools of higher learning in Constantinople and in the Orient, and also in Italy and in other kingdoms, schools where they may study freely and read what they wish.

Ninth: Let us just take ourselves as an example: The two emperors Diocletian and Maximian issued a common mandate in the eighth year of their reign, wherein they decreed that all Christian books be burned. But once each local magistrate began a search for Christian books in his region, the imperial commissar Magnianus approached Felix, the Bishop of Thibiuka (near Carthage) and Januarius, the priest, and also Fortunatus and Septimius, as the people likely to be best informed about the whereabouts of the books, each in his own region. They replied: "It is written: Thou shallt not give that which is Holy to the hounds nor toss pearls to the pigs"—and they rather died than show him where he could find the books.

Nevertheless, all the Christian books that were not hidden were destroyed. And following the death of the two aforementioned emperors, heretics emerged and wrote other books; they gave them titles with the names of saints, as if, thereby, to pretend sanction, titles like: *The Gospel According to Thaddeus, The Gospel According to the Apostle Thomas, The Gospel According to the Apostle Barnabas, The Gospel According to Bartholemew, The Gospel According to the Apostle Andrew* and many other books, all of which are listed in the canonical law *(15. dis. c. Sancta romana ecclesia. §. Quae vero.)*.

This practice continued until, finally, they had once again retrieved all the old books hidden throughout the entire Roman Empire, in the East and in the West, which books were then perused and appraised in subsequent Church councils. We cannot, however, establish that as a consequence of the destruction of Christian books, there were fewer Christians than there otherwise might have been had the books not been burned. In fact, the contrary is true, the Christian Church grew all the more in number and strength in the years that followed. And this is precisely what would happen here too: If the Jews perceived a threat to their holiest possession, then they would wish all the more ardently to die as Jews, in the belief that they were holy martyrs, and thereby, exhorting their women and children to hold all the more fervently to their faith.

Therefore, we are prohibited by canonical law *(c. sicut iudae. ex de iu.)* from confiscating the Jews' possessions, whether money or valuable things encompassed under the rubric of *"pecunia" (1. q. 3 totum)*. And whoever acts in defiance of this decree shall be relieved of his worldly honors and his position or be banned (i.e., excommunicated), until he has made sufficient recompense to the injured party. Now it is a fundamental principle of law that no one be banned, except for a mortal sin *(11. q. 3. c. Nemo)*. For if it is a sin, then it does not serve God's purpose.

This Church law likewise applies to all kings and emperors, in that they too are Christians. Imperial Law, moreover, adopted this statute *(in 1. Christianis. C. de paga.),* and specified, furthermore, that the injured party be recompensed by the perpetrator at double the value of his loss. And any high officials or magistrates who knowingly condone such a crime should, likewise, be punished, as if they themselves had been the perpetrators. For if the Jews keep the peace, then we should also leave them in peace *(dicto. .1. Christianis).*

All this is done precisely so that they cannot maintain that we wish to pressure or force them to accept our faith. It is for this reason that the holy Apostle Paul writes to the Thessalonians (1 Thessalonians 4:10ff.): "We beseech you, brethren...that ye study to be quiet...that ye may walk honestly toward them that are without, and that ye may have lack of nothing." That is to say: We should not bother those who are not Christians or covet anything that belongs to them. We must not, therefore, take and baptize their children without the parents' permission *(glo. in ca. iudaeorum filios 28. q. 1).* This view is upheld by teachers of the Holy Scripture, as, for instance, by Augustine of Ancona in his *Summa* concerning ecclesiastical force, *quaestio* 25. From this we may conclude that we also may not take their books away from them against their will, for books are as dear to some as their children. Do we not in our common usage follow the parlance of the poets, for whom the books they write are in a manner of speaking children of the soul! Here too, we must bear in mind: If our purpose in confiscating a Jew's books is precisely to bring him over to the Christian faith, then such an action would be tantamount to force *(glo. super ver. licentiatum in fi. 45. dis. c. Qui syncera)*.

Since, however, our most gracious Sire, the Roman Emperor, also instructed your Lordship to solicit expert opinions in what way, with what justification, and by what actions this matter had best be approached and resolved—and seeing as I myself have, herewith, undertaken the charge given me by your Lordship on His Majesty's behalf, to weigh in and offer my advice—truly, in my humble opinion, I can recommend no better course of action than the following. For God's sake and that of our Christian Faith, let His Imperial Majesty direct the schools of higher learning in Germany to hire two lecturers for a ten-year term at each of its universities; these lecturers should be qualified and responsible for teaching and supervising instruction in the Hebrew language, according to a dictate of Pope Clementine *(sub titulo: de magistris, prima)*. To this end, I urge that the Jews residing in our land put their books at our disposal as a neighborly loan—naturally with appropriate compensation and the assurance that great care will be taken to avoid any damage to the same—until such time as we have succeeded through printing or transcription to supply our own books. Should such a course of action be undertaken, I have no doubt but that in a very few years our students will be so conversant in the Hebrew language that they will be ready and able by means of logical and friendly discourse to gently lead the Jews into our camp, while holding to the dictates of canonical law *(c. qui sincera et. c. de iudae. 45. dis.)*, wherein the following is expressly stated: "Whoever sets himself the task, in good conscience, of leading those outside

Christendom to the true faith, let him proceed with gentle words and not with a harsh tongue, so that resentment not drive away those whose spirit might well be induced by kindness and reason to turn from error. And as to those who would do otherwise, and seek, under the guise of everyday motives, to shake them [the Jews] from their faith, one may conclude that in so doing they are not advancing God's interests, but their own. We should, therefore, deal with them [the Jews] in such a way as to so move them with logical arguments and gentleness of manner that they would rather join us and not flee from us, so that with God's help and the testimony of their own books, we may succeed in converting them to the cause of our Mother, the Christian Church."

This is, more or less, the gist of the canonical law *(dicto. ca. qui sincera),* upon which I base my opinion concerning the treatment of the Jews in this regard. And the canon, entitled *"de iudaeis" (ea. dis.)* states furthermore: "Concerning the Jews, the Holy Council has commanded that, henceforth, no person be forcibly coerced to accept our Faith: For whomever God wants, to him shall He be merciful, and whomsoever He wishes He hardens against Him. Therefore, salvation cannot be forced upon those people unwilling to receive it, but rather, only received by those of good will, so that the spirit and letter of the law remain unblemished."

From the two aforementioned articles of law, the "Clementine" and the "Distinction of the Decree," we may derive the conclusive judgment in this entire matter, namely: That we should not burn the Jews' books, and that through logical discourse, we should convince them with gentle persuasion and kindness and with God's help to accept our Faith.

Most noble Lord, gracious Sire! I duly declare that I do, hereby, submit my written word and my recommendation as a humble sovereign of Your Lordship, my Archbishop, and that I have knowingly written nothing save that which is sanctioned by Your Lordship and the Holy Christian Church.

To this do I solemnly swear, and sign,

Respectfully, Ever Your Lordship's loyal subject and willing servant.

Dated: Stuttgart, 6 October, Anno 1510

Notes

1. Né Solomon ben Levi, a Christian convert, appointed in 1415 as Bishop of Burgos.

2. Pico della Mirandola, Italian Humanist, 1463–94.

3. German-born Dominican scholar of Hebrew, 1434–83.

4. Reference to Johannes Pfefferkorn's *Judenfeind,* 1509.

5. Converted Jew and former rabbi, Dominican professor of Hebrew in Barcelona, circa 1220–86.

6. By Magister Alfonsus of Burgos, son of a converted Jew, translator, philosopher and poet, named Bishop of Burgos, 1386–1456.

7. See note 1.

8. Dominican, Hebrew scholar, author of books and sermons against the Jews, 1434–83.

9. Spanish Franciscan of Jewish ancestry, died 1469.

10. French Franciscan, circa 1270–1349.

11. Né Moses, Spanish Christian convert, 1062–1106.

12. Alfonsus of Burgos, son of Jewish convert, translator, philosopher, poet, diplomat, named Bishop of Burgos, circa 1386–1456.

13. A learned Christian convert, translator and biblical commentator, named Archbishop of Toledo, died 1166.

14. Author of a popular 13th-century book of aphorisms.

15. Egyptian Christian hermit, 345–410.

16. Greek Christian theologian, 185–254.

17. Founder of the Monophysitic heresy.

18. Bishop of Constantinople, founder of Nestorian heresy.

19. Teacher at the Court of Constantinople, 491–518.

20. Noted grammarian, born circa 359.

21. Roman grammarian, teacher of St. Jerome.

22. Noted French talmudist, circa 1030–1105.

23. Spanish exegete and kabbalist, circa 1195–1270.

24. Noted fifteenth-century scholar, mathematician, kabbalist.

25. Hebrew grammarians.

26. Hebrew linguist, exegete, circa 1160–1235.

27. Hebrew grammarian.

28. French Franciscan, circa 1270–1349, employed the work of Jewish scholars, in particular, Rashi, for his biblical exegeses.

29. Bartolo da Sassoferrata, 1314–57, Italian jurist familiar with Hebrew, known, in particular, for his commentaries on civil law regarding the Jews.

30. Roman historian.

31. Alfonsus de Spina, Spanish Franciscan theologian of Jewish parentage, died 1469.

other volumes in this series

Stepping Stones to Further Jewish-Christian Relations: An Unabridged Collection of Christian Documents, compiled by Helga Croner (A Stimulus Book, 1977).

Helga Croner and Leon Klenicki, editors, *Issues in the Jewish-Christian Dialogue: Jewish Perspectives on Covenant, Mission and Witness* (A Stimulus Book, 1979).

Clemens Thoma, *A Christian Theology of Judaism* (A Stimulus Book, 1980).

Helga Croner, Leon Klenicki and Lawrence Boadt, C.S.P., editors, *Biblical Studies: Meeting Ground of Jews and Christians* (A Stimulus Book, 1980).

Pawlikowski, John T., O.S.M., *Christ in the Light of the Christian-Jewish Dialogue* (A Stimulus Book, 1982).

Leon Klenicki and Gabe Huck, editors, *Spirituality and Prayer: Jewish and Christian Understandings* (A Stimulus Book, 1983).

Edward Flannery, *The Anguish of the Jews* (A Stimulus Book, 1985).

More Stepping Stones to Jewish-Christian Relations: An Unabridged Collection of Christian Documents 1975–1983, compiled by Helga Croner (A Stimulus Book, 1985).

Clemens Thoma and Michael Wyschogrod, editors, *Understanding Scripture: Explorations of Jewish and Christian Traditions of Interpretation* (A Stimulus Book, 1987).

Bernard J. Lee, S.M., *The Galilean Jewishness of Jesus* (A Stimulus Book, 1988).

Clemens Thoma and Michael Wyschogrod, editors, *Parable and Story in Judaism and Christianity* (A Stimulus Book, 1989).

Eugene J. Fisher and Leon Klenicki, editors, *In Our Time: The Flowering of Jewish-Catholic Dialogue* (A Stimulus Book, 1990).

Leon Klenicki, editor, *Toward A Theological Encounter* (A Stimulus Book, 1991).

David Burrell and Yehezkel Landau, editors, *Voices from Jerusalem* (A Stimulus Book, 1991).

John Rousmaniere, *A Bridge to Dialogue: The Story of Jewish-Christian Relations;* edited by James A. Carpenter and Leon Klenicki (A Stimulus Book, 1991).

Michael E. Lodahl, *Shekhinah/Spirit* (A Stimulus Book, 1992).

George M. Smiga, *Pain and Polemic: Anti-Judaism in the Gospels* (A Stimulus Book, 1992).

Eugene J. Fisher, editor, *Interwoven Destinies: Jews and Christians Through the Ages* (A Stimulus Book, 1993).

Anthony Kenny, *Catholics, Jews and the State of Israel* (A Stimulus Book, 1993).

Eugene J. Fisher, editor, *Visions of the Other: Jewish and Christian Theologians Assess the Dialogue* (A Stimulus Book, 1995).

Leon Klenicki and Geoffrey Wigoder, editors, *A Dictionary of the Jewish-Christian Dialogue* (Expanded Edition), (A Stimulus Book, 1995).

Frank E. Eakin, Jr., *What Price Prejudice?: Christian Antisemitism in America* (A Stimulus Book, 1998).

Ekkehard Schuster & Reinhold Boschert-Kimmig, *Hope Against Hope: Johann Baptist Metz and Elie Wiesel Speak Out on the Holocaust* (A Stimulus Book, 1999).

Mary C. Boys, *Has God Only One Blessing?: Judaism as a Source of Christian Understanding* (A Stimulus Book, 2000).

STIMULUS BOOKS are developed by Stimulus Foundation, a not-for-profit organization, and are published by Paulist Press. The Foundation wishes to further the publication of scholarly books on Jewish and Christian topics that are of importance to Judaism and Christianity.

Stimulus Foundation was established by an erstwhile refugee from Nazi Germany who intends to contribute with these publications to the improvement of communication between Jews and Christians.

Books for publication in this Series will be selected by a committee of the Foundation, and offers of manuscripts and works in progress should be addressed to:

Stimulus Foundation
c/o Paulist Press
997 Macarthur Boulevard
Mahwah, N.J. 07430
www.paulistpress.com